Successful Singing Auditions

Gillyanne Kayes
& Jeremy Fisher

A & C Black • London

First published in 2002 by
A & C Black Publishers Limited
37 Soho Square, London W1D 3QZ

© 2002 Gillyanne Kayes and Jeremy Fisher

ISBN 0 7136 5807 X

A CIP catalogue record for this book is available from the
British Library.

Typeset in 10 on 12pt Sabon

A & C Black uses paper produced with elemental chlorine-free pulp,
harvested from managed sustainable forests.

Printed and bound in Great Britain by CPD (Wales)

Successful Singing Auditions

Contents

Acknowledgements   vi

1   The Audition Arena.   01
2   Who's There?.   08
3   Your Voice.   19
4   Casting Your Voice.   25
5   What Makes You Special?   36
6   Know Your Genre!.   50
7   What Is Style?   58
8   Your Portfolio   74
9   Conscious Learning   81
10 Making Decisions.   94
11 Making Cuts   108
12 Memorising   115
13 Audition Countdown   125
14 At The Audition.   132

Appendix A   141

Index   148
Index of Song Titles   150
Song Credits   154

Acknowledgements

Books are not written on their own. Our thanks to all the actors with whom we have worked over a period of many years, in workshops, productions, and in the studio.

A number of people have kindly read and commented on chapters or helped us with queries. Thanks to Dinah Harris, Jayne Comins, Andrew Wade, Colin Sell, Mary Hammond and Fiona Sinnott.

Actors who were interviewed for the *FOAL* PROCESS include Rebecca Deren, Jamie Turnbull and Nikola Monfort. Our thanks to you. Also to MDs, agents and casting directors who took part in our audition survey including Michael England, Martin Lowe, Pippa Ailion and Hilary Gagan.

Special thanks are due to Richard Lipton for advice on the Diction Score in Chapter 9 and to Elisabeth Stirling for advice on NLP terminology in Chapter 12.

To Ana Sanderson for patience, accuracy, support and tact in the editing process.

Last but by no means least to all our friends, who have endured neglect during the months of writing and are still there for us.

Chapter 1

The Audition Arena

Auditioning is a tricky business and one of the hardest things an actor has to do. Everyone has to go through it, and some, it seems, survive better than others. Remember the famous scene in the film *Tootsie* where Dustin Hoffman says – 'I can do taller'? This book is about doing better auditions *and* surviving the experience. It will enable you to regard auditioning as a process, not an end gain, and to accept it as part of your life as an actor. In addition, a singing audition has its own unique features that are sometimes missed by those who attempt it. Our aim is to reveal these features and show you how to use them to your advantage. Will this guarantee you success as an actor? Of course not, but you will be more likely to get through that vital first round because you will be better prepared and understand the standard that is expected. You will also begin to enjoy your auditions and to use them creatively.

So an audition is a kind of performance. What makes it different from any other kind of performance?

1. The audience hasn't paid and they won't applaud. Often they will give you no feedback of any kind.
2. The house lights are up; the audience is visible and apparently uninterested, perhaps talking.
3. There is no set, you are not in costume, you have no props and there are no other actors on stage.
4. You enter the arena as yourself and must change from self to character onstage, in full view, and back again when you have finished the piece.

In addition, at a singing audition:

5. There is music and you have to sing. Generally we do not burst into song in conversational speech or when reporting events or in moments of heightened emotion. Songs serve many functions when used in a theatrical context, enabling the audience to experience the action on other levels. Spontaneous singing does have a place in our lives but the audition isn't one of those places. If you are not sure what we mean, just think about the difference between singing '*You'll Never Walk Alone*' at a football match and

1

singing it at an audition.

6. There is a pianist. You do not know if this person is a friend or foe, and you have to create a performance with them without rehearsal or even a prior meeting.

7. There is a piano or keyboard. Perhaps the pianist is good but the piano is awful and out of tune; perhaps it is the other way around and the pianist cannot play your music. (Note that most auditions do not allow backing tracks; the panel wants to see a live performance.)

You will realise by now that we have used the word arena for a specific purpose, because auditioning really can feel like being thrown to the lions if you are unprepared for the experience. However, when you have understood the process and your part in it, auditioning will become yet another performing arena – it is just a special type of performance.

Let's look at some of these audition features more closely.

Why an audition isn't like any other type of performance

At an audition the panel is the audience and they are there to do a job. Their job is to find the right person to fill the gap in their company or show. Because of this they must listen and watch critically. This is an essential difference between an audition and a normal public performance. Audiences will exercise their critical faculties, and it is essential for the arts that they do so. However, their prime motivation for attending a theatre performance is to be entertained, uplifted, moved, shocked – taken out of themselves in some way. While the panel may enjoy your performance, they cannot afford the luxury of staying in that mode because of the job they are there to do. They must see from watching you whether or not you can be comfortable in the performing arena; they will know within the first bar of your song if you can sing, and they will probably know after the next bar whether or not you are at the appropriate standard. Audiences also respond at a performance – with silence, with palpable attention, with laughter, and finally with applause. You do not get a hand at audition, though you may be thanked. This means that you are deprived of one of your main sources of feedback, and it is important to keep focused on what you are there to do.

So what is *your* job at the audition? You may be surprised to hear that it is not to give your best performance. The job in hand is to give a clear and accurate picture of yourself: to demonstrate to the panel your professional level and your skill as a performer. Only with this information can the panel place you. We have found that many good singers are not successful at auditions because they are unable to give the panel a clear picture of themselves. This happens most often when the actor is working for the audition from the outside in: looking for the right song for the audition that will impress the panel and get him or her that part in that show. The more of these 'rights' that you pile on the audition, the further away you get from the product you are demonstrating to the panel – YOU. So the trick is not to audition for the job – it is to do the job of auditioning.

Moving into character

At an audition you come on as yourself, must move into character for the song and then come out of character. This is very important for the panel because they need to get a feel for you as a person, in and out of character, and how smooth the change is. They want to know what you will be like to work with, and they will need to assess whether or not the performance you have just given matches up with your CV. Your CV tells them what you have done so far and about the level they can expect you to sustain in a long run, i.e. your current professional level.

Features of a singing audition

Why isn't a singing audition the same as singing at a football match? At the football match you are carried on a tide of emotion (the same could be said of some hymn singing). At an audition (or any performance of a solo song) you have to find the motivation *yourself* for using the medium of music for whatever it is you have to say. Within the context of a show, if you are on stage alone and singing a song, there are events that have led up to this moment to prepare both you and the audience for the song. This doesn't happen at auditions. Using the Five W's – who, what, why, where, and when – in an audition, the answer to the last question is always now.[1] Whatever it is that you have to say through the song, whatever effect you want to have on the person or people you are singing it to, you are doing it right now – in the moment.

The pianist

What difficulties might you experience through having to work with a pianist you have never met before? Horror stories about pianists at auditions are legion and we all feel indignant when we hear them, but

[1]The Five W's see *Singing and The Actor* pp 170–171

the bottom line is that you are doing the audition, not the pianist. It is up to you to make sure that your music is properly prepared and marked up, to communicate your needs clearly to the pianist (the map of the song, tempi and so on) and to take charge if his/her rendition is not quite what you expect. Remember that whatever the condition of the piano itself, or the pianist, everyone else doing the audition that day will be in the same boat and the panel will be aware of it. You do not have to do a poor audition because of the pianist. In these situations you must take charge by using your own judgement. If you can hear (from outside) that the pianist is really bad, produce the song that you have prepared for just this kind of occasion. It should be a song that you do well and that has been transposed into a simple key such as C, D or G (major or minor). We will talk about this in more detail in Chapters 8 and 13 of the book.

Understanding the target for each type of audition is vital to successful auditioning. Here is a breakdown of the key stages:

1. The Open Call

Your targets are to:
i   show that you can sing.
ii show that you have learned and prepared your music (many people do not understand how to do this properly).
iii show that you are viable as a stage performer.
iv show that you are at a suitable professional level.
v   show that you have understood the brief of the audition as advertised.
vi get called back or kept on file for auditioning on another occasion or for another company.

2. The first private audition

Your targets are to:
i   get through to the recall.
ii demonstrate that your skills as a performer are at the level required for the show and for your potential place in it (ensemble, cover, swing, named part, lead).
iii allow the panel to get a feel for you as a person.

3. The first recall

You may be asked to repeat your songs from last time, to sing something new, or to learn something from the show. Let's assume you have been asked to learn some music from the show. You will know from this whether or not the panel is looking at you for ensemble, possible cover or a role. Your targets are to:

i show that you have learned and can sing the music to the required standard and in the right style. This may include details such as the range of the song and voice quality. Sometimes the panel will really like you and want you for a particular role that actually isn't right for your voice. The recall system is their way of finding this out.

ii enable the panel to see more layers of your ability as an actor; now they will see you playing a different role, and they will be able to find out much more about your suitability for the place they are looking to fill.

Sometimes the first and second recall happens because the panel really liked your performance but for some reason couldn't 'place' you. They need more information, and calling you back is the only way they can get it. In our experience there are only two reasons why the recalls run and run:

1. *You* are not giving them a clear enough message. Sometimes they really want to give you the role, but you are not showing them something that they require.

2. *They* are not clear about what they want. The reasons for this can range from the company not knowing (yet) who is actually leaving the show, to not knowing what the producer, director or choreographer wants, to not knowing how the show itself is going to evolve. Whatever the reason, the result for you is the same; it is important not to get demoralised as you go through this process.

Note that you can only be in control of your own part in this process. Otherwise you have two choices: sweat it out or pull out. It is OK for you to say: 'This is not right for me, I will put my energy elsewhere.' The recall system in fact benefits you because it enables you to find your true level and whether or not the job is right for you.

So you will only get the job if the panel are convinced that you are the most appropriate person to do it. Sometimes this process of choosing can be very lengthy; it is not a case of just one audition. Just like the job interview, the audition is about shortlisting the real 'possibles' and then finding from them the best match for the needs of the production. This may include matching you with other members of the company, or it may include factors such as your star quality or professional profile, which might enhance the show's commercial viability.

Measuring your success

A successful audition is not only about signing the contract at the end of the process. That is a bonus. What are the hallmarks of a successful audition?

1. You leave the arena knowing that you have shown something of yourself, both in and out of character.
2. You are satisfied that you have given a good account of yourself.
3. You did justice to the material that you took to the audition.
4. The tools of your trade – your voice and your body – were fit to present your performance.
5. You interacted well with the pianist (either you worked together or you led him to the performance you wanted).
6. You interacted appropriately with the panel as yourself.
7. You were not thrown by unusual happenings.
8. You did the best you could *under the circumstances you found yourself in*; no-one can do more.

You do not need feedback from anyone else to know these things.

Here are some real life stories about auditions.

A singer-dancer was called to do an audition for a long running West End show. A very experienced performer who had done a lot of West End shows, she came back feeling very disappointed about the audition even though she felt sure that she had sung well. When asked why she said it was because there was a lot of talking and paper rustling during her audition, and that the panel had looked 'worried'. She was quite used to the former but not the latter. She wondered if she had been doing something wrong and consequently was beginning to question her judgement. She was not recalled for that audition. Some time later she was told by a member of the panel that she had, in fact, sung very well and that this was precisely the reason why they had looked worried. It turned out that the panel had been worried about offering her the job (a place in the ensemble) as they felt that she was too good and would be insulted. She was actually in the process of upping her level from dancer-singer to singer-dancer, and the audition that she gave demonstrated this. Therefore it was a successful audition.

A young singer-actor was sent for private audition for a West End show. She was complimented on her performance at the audition and was told that she would definitely be recalled. Her second experience was not so good: the panel seemed disinterested and even stopped her halfway through her song. From their response she naturally felt that she had disappointed in some way. However, when she left the auditorium she was asked to wait and was then introduced to the producer of another show who had come in that day to hear her. He told her that she would be perfect for a role in his show (a long running West End musical) and that he would like her to audition whenever she was available.

A singer-actor went through a number of recalls for a production at the South Bank and wondered why she was called back again and again. This was neither a long running show nor a new one, both situations where the recalls may be numerous. It transpired that the director was looking for something that she had not yet revealed. When she turned up for the final audition in a bad temper and demonstrating a bit of attitude, it transpired that it was exactly this quality the director felt the role required.

All three of these are examples of successful auditions, even though it was only in the last case that the actor was offered the job.

What about using auditioning as a learning experience? To answer this question, work out first what it is that you are trying to learn. Our advice is never to go to a private audition unless you believe you are ready to do the job that you are being auditioned for. Going to an open call for the experience of auditioning is OK so long as you can meet the brief of the audition as advertised. If the brief isn't clear (and it isn't always) then get your agent to find out or call the casting director or company manager, saying that you need more information. If you are the wrong standard, take the wrong type of song or are nowhere near the casting type required, you are wasting your and the panel's time by turning up for the audition. Not only that, the only thing you will experience is an unproductive audition.

We could summarise the content of this chapter in two points:

1. When going to any audition, be sure of what it is that you have to offer before you go.
2. If you are doing the audition to get feedback about yourself, your skills or your professional level, don't go because you will not get it!

Chapter 2

Who's There?

In the previous chapter we looked at the auditioning arena: what happens there and what is expected of you. Now we need to look more closely at who is in the arena.

1. The panel. This may consist of various people depending on the purpose of the audition. It could be a casting director and one other person. If you are auditioning for an agency, it might be one person only. At the other end of the scale the panel might consist of the producer, the composer, the musical director, the casting director, the director, the staff director, the choreographer and the company manager.
2. The pianist.
3. You.

The demands of a modern world are reflected in the need for actors to be more and more versatile. Whether this is a good or bad thing is not within the scope of this book. Accepting it as reality means that actors are under a lot of pressure to be skilled in a number of areas and to be able to perform in different genres. There are many different types of audition but, in all cases, you are the common factor.

This brings us to a key concept in this book.

Your level of competence

It is extremely important to be able to assess your level of competence accurately and honestly. We are not meaning to imply by this that an actor should not challenge him or herself – far from it. However, the audition is not the place to do it. It is not a good idea to audition for a job that is beyond your current level of competence. The occasion of itself is enough of a challenge, and you will have plenty of opportunities to challenge yourself when you have got the job. There is a saying in business that we can be promoted to our level of *in-*competence: in a company environment, a person who does well at their job is usually rewarded with promotion to the next level – where they have to learn again. They will finally reach their level of competence and will be rewarded with yet another promotion. In this job they are unable to shine. They have now reached their level of incompetence, and, except in extraordinary circumstances, they will not be demoted. Nor will they be promoted; they will merely be unhappy.

We think it is really important for actors to understand what it means to be promoted or offered a job that is beyond their current level of competence or professional skill. This can happen in the case of established performers who may not be experienced singers, or not experienced in a particular genre. They are already at a high professional level, have a high profile, and the producers are prepared to take a gamble on their singing skills. If this is you, make sure that you use the recall system to find out if you really want to do the job. Actors in this situation can find the reality of doing the show far more unpleasant than the auditioning. If you are learning a new skill (such as singing) on the job, you will find it difficult to pay attention to anything else except that skill, and the acting skills that you do have may suffer in consequence. So may your confidence.

Gillyanne Here are a couple of examples from my studio. A young performer was fortunate enough to move straight from college into a West End lead. Though a talented singer and performer she did not have the life experience to withstand some of the professional rivalry she met with in the real world. Another young performer went into a prestigious musical production early on in her career. A talented actress, she also sang well but had been cast in a role that she did not find easy to sing (though it was perfect for her as an actress). Each of these performers experienced a loss of confidence and I could sense it in their lessons as they became more guarded. If you have to go out on stage every night, you do not want the additional strain of having to think about something new that your vocal coach has suggested, even if in the long run it would improve your performance. There was a happy ending to both these stories. The first performer sought jobs out of the West End, getting valuable field experience until she felt ready to go back; the second negotiated with her agent not to put her up for musicals for a while and concentrated on building a career as a classical actress.

Ideally your professional level and your skills and competence levels should match. Incidentally this is one of the reasons why you have an agent. Good agents are not there just to get you auditions; they can advise you about short and long term projects for your career and give you the honest feedback that you do not always get from your peers.

In order to assess your level of competence you need to look at the *type* of singing work you do (or aspire to do) and *where* you do it.

Level of competence 1: categories of singers

There are six categories of singer that we have identified. Performers in these categories do jobs right across the board of musical theatre and theatre with music. You will fall into one of them, or maybe more. You can also move across the categories by doing work to improve your skills. Note that when we refer to 'an actor' in the text we mean a performer who may belong to any one of these categories.

1. Actor-singer

Actor-singer means that you are an actor first and that singing is one of the skills listed on your CV. You will be able to hold a tune and will probably find it easiest to sing when on stage and in character. You won't feel yourself to be a strong singer, though, in fact, with a little bit of input you will be perfectly competent. In an ideal world any actor would be able to meet the requirements of this category. Here are the kinds of performance that may require an actor who does not consider himself as a 'singer' to sing:

- Pantomime
- A Brecht play
- A Shakespeare play (the music may be in a period or modern style)
- A television drama
- A film about musicians or singers (the Mike Leigh film *Topsy Turvey*)
- Devised TIE shows
- An original play that has perhaps one song in it for a particular character (Adam in *The Four Seasons* by Arnold Wesker)
- A play that is using music as a backdrop to the action and for scene changes (rather like a film but live), e.g. Cheek by Jowl's *Duchess of Malfi* and London Bubble Theatre Company's *Lords and Ladies*.

Unlike the songs in musical theatre, songs in actor-singer productions generally do not advance the plot. Their function is to get the audience to think about the action in a different way: either to distance from the emotional response to the action, or to allow it to be experienced on a deeper level. Bertolt Brecht used songs to distance the audience from the action and to teach; Dennis Potter used song to comment on the action in his television play *The Singing Detective*. Songs in pantomime are there mostly to engage the audience directly and also to enhance the feel-good factor. In Shakespeare's plays, songs serve a variety of functions: allowing for scene changes, aiding a change of mood, commenting on the action (Fool's songs in *King Lear*), or enabling the audience to respond to the action on a different level ('*Fear no more the heat o' the sun*' from *Cymbeline*).

What do the panel need to hear from you in your audition as an actor-singer? First and foremost that you can hold a tune and that you will be able to fill the space as required. Many plays with music will not be miked; they are a very different affair from the high-tech sound system that is part of some musicals. You may even be performing in the open air, which presents its own difficulties for projection. The musical director may want to check out your range and test whether you can sing harmonies. You might even be asked to learn a few lines to sing along with him, to show that you can hold your own in this situation. Make sure that you find out if this particular skill is required before you go. Some actors are 'one song' actors, i.e. they learn new song material very slowly. If this is you, take a tape recorder with you to rehearsals and do plenty of homework on the note learning between rehearsals. If you follow the guidelines in Chapter 8 for learning a song fast, you will make more efficient use of your practice time.

What you will need at the audition
1. For some actor-singer auditions you could be asked to bring a piece that is not musical theatre material. Standards of the Thirties, Forties and Fifties are good for this type of audition. These songs can often be played in a number of different ways and their musical style adjusts easily to a more modern idiom if required. Make sure that you have the sheet music in your key.
2. Yet another type of audition will require you to sing a cappella (unaccompanied). This isn't just because the company concerned wants to save money on paying an audition pianist – it's also a great way to see if you really can hold a tune. Have something ready for this eventuality: something that reads well unaccompanied, such as a traditional folk song, an Elizabethan lute song, or a short song that is melodic and rhythmically straightforward. Avoid doing your favourite pop song, particularly if it is dependant on the instrumental backing.
3. The pantomime audition is almost a category in itself. Some companies will write original music for the show each year. In this case you are lucky because, if you are chosen at audition, the musical director is likely to write something for you that will suit your voice and your abilities. Depending on the style of writing,

you will be asked to bring one song that demonstrates your vocal range, perhaps in a particular genre, e.g. a pop ballad, a traditional folk song, music hall and so on.

4. Alternatively a touring company might use a click track for popular cover numbers that make up the music for the show. Sometimes the songs chosen will vary enormously in style. From the point of view of your audition, that really doesn't matter; just take any song that you can sing with confidence and put over well. If you are a one song actor, avoid the pantomime until you have done some work on your learning skills; singing with a click track requires a good sense of rhythm and performing up to ten shows a week is extremely demanding. Remember too that your audience will be a vocal one!

2. Dancer-singer

Dancer-singers will have trained primarily in dance, probably at one of the dance academies. Often they will have had some singing input in their training, but it will be minimal on the technical side. We have found that dancer-singers are often well prepared in the portfolio department, but not in the vocal one. However, dancers are generally very disciplined and respond quickly to accurate technical information, so it is not difficult to bring yourself up to this standard if you feel you can dance but are a non-singer. Dancer-singers are often employed as ensemble in musicals that involve choreographed dance routines. Sometimes the ensemble will consist of dancer-singers and singer-dancers; it all depends on the relative complexity of the choreography and the chorus work. If you are unsure about going to an audition that requires singing and dance, remember the song 'Dance Ten, Looks Three' from *A Chorus Line*. Your dance will need to be a ten, but your voice can be less, say a five. Do not go to a dance audition if you are dance five, voice eight; you will not get through the dance routine and may not get to sing at all if the routine is the first part of the audition, which is generally the case. However, if you are dance eight and voice three it just might be worth your while going along.

Here are some examples of productions that use dancer-singers in the ensemble: *Me and My Girl, Oklahoma!, Starlight Express, Miss Saigon, Copacabana, Cats* (smaller roles, known as the kittens), and *Martin Guerre*.

Vocally you need to be skilled enough to learn a tune quickly and to sing your audition song with style. How you look when you deliver the song – your presentation – will also be important. Your voice is

less important. You must be able to sing in tune but you do not need
to have a voice that fills the theatre. Your range does not need to be
large: the musical director will be looking for singers who can cover
the range in each part. There is one important difference between the
actor-singer and dancer-singer: you must be able to hold your own
line in part-singing. People often think that it is easier to hold a part
if you are not singing on your own, but that is only the case in unison
songs. If you are singing harmonies then you must be experienced in
learning them and maintaining them. Do you find it easy to sing in
tune? Generally the part-singing in dance ensembles is simple, but you
will not be able to do it if tuning is an issue for you.

What you will need at the audition
1. Make sure you know your working range and have it marked on
   your CV (resumé).
2. Have songs in your portfolio that are short and that enable the
   panel to hear quickly how well you can sing. (Gershwin refrains
   are ideal for this.)
3. Make sure that you can cover the book musicals (Rodgers and
   Hart, Rodgers and Hammerstein) as well as the more modern
   dance musicals such as *Fame, Saturday Night Fever* and *Grease*.
4. An upbeat pop number is also a good idea.

3. Actor-musician

This is quite a special category. What makes you different as an
actor musician from all the other categories is your level of
musicianship and your instrumental skill. Actor-musicians can
cover a range of jobs from musical director in small shows to
playing an instrument on stage and performing in the show, to
writing and devising the musical content of a show to enabling
others to play very basic lines on instruments. Not all actor-
musicians are singers, though in our opinion they should be vocally
skilled to the same level as actor-singers. Actor-musicians are
usually trained actors with instrumental skills, who are often
interested in writing or devising music for shows. There are now
courses in the drama colleges and universities as well as course
modules for actors who are interested in training for this type of
work.
    If you are an actor-musician you will be able to read music and
learn quickly. You will play at least one instrument to a high standard
(often grade exams are indicated in the specifications for audition).
You will be able to sing in tune and hold a part. In addition you may

have writing and teaching skills or be able to operate a sound system.

Here are some examples of shows requiring actor-musician: *Return to the Forbidden Planet, Buddy* (some roles), *Threepenny Opera* (where the musicians are on stage and form part of the cast), smaller scale touring productions where the music is provided by the actors e.g. London Bubble, *The Best of Times* (in this show about the music of Jerry Herman the pianist is required to perform on stage and take part in a simple tap number and a solo song).

What you will need at the audition
1. The requirements for actor-musician auditions will often be quite specific, so you will need to make sure you can meet these before going.
2. It may be more important to demonstrate your standard of musicianship than to show you have a good voice. You might easily be asked one week to sing a rock 'n' roll number and on the following week a classical song.
3. You will almost certainly be required to harmonise if you are singing in the show. Be ready to improvise harmonies at the audition either with the pianist or with other actors who may be present.
4. It is useful to have a working range of two octaves plus if you are an actor-musician: it makes you more employable. Make sure that your CV details your singing range; men should include their falsetto range as well.
5. You may be asked to learn a short piece of music or to read at sight using your main instrument. Be ready!
6. Make sure you have songs in your repertoire that show you are capable of working in a number of styles. This could include a Brecht/Weill or Brecht Eisler song, a music hall or vaudeville song, a setting of a Shakespearean or other text (modern, traditional or written by yourself), a song from a book musical, a song from a contemporary musical (either the verismo or concept category, and a pop song from a tribute musical).[1] At least one of the songs should show off your voice type and range. One song should be unaccompanied or arranged so that you can accompany yourself.

4. *Singer-dancer*

In a dance musical it is the singer-dancers who will take the lead and supporting roles. More often than not, all members of the cast will

[1]For a detailed breakdown of the categories mentioned, see Chapter 6

dance the ensemble numbers, so your dance skills must be on a level with the dancer-singers if you aspire to this category. Your singing, on the other hand, must be of a much higher standard than that of a dancer-singer. If you want to be cast in lead roles you will also have to be comfortable using the medium of text. Shows using singer-dancers include *Sweet Charity*, *Chicago*, *Fosse*, *Grease* and *West Side Story*.

It is quite common for dancer-singers to retrain once they have been performing for ten–fifteen years, so that they can continue their careers as singer-dancers. Like the singer-actor you should have a working vocal range of two octaves, enjoy the medium of song and have a strong vocal presence.

What you will need at the audition
1. Like the singer-actor, you need to know your genre and take music that is stylistically appropriate to the audition.
2. You should have songs that suit your voice type and vocal range and that show different aspects of your performing persona: ballad, character, comedy, point, uptempo and so on.
3. You need to show that you can hold the audience's attention both physically and vocally.

5. Singer-actor

A singer-actor will include performing in musical theatre as part of his/her career plan. It is essential if you are planning to do this that singing is a comfortable medium of communication for you. Please note that it is not enough that you enjoy listening to vocal music to come into this category. Many actors have good voices and can sing well but do not enjoy the medium: these actors are happier in the actor-singer category because spoken text is their most comfortable mode. This is not to say that, in the course of your career or training, you might not move from one category to another, provided you can acquire the necessary skills.

You will be vocally skilled with a good range (two octaves plus) and able to learn notes quickly. More importantly you will be able to mirror psychological changes within a song through your singing voice and will be able to change your voice for different characterisations. In addition you will be able to sing in a range of voice qualities so that you can move from one style of musical to another. For example, you will be able to cope with a part in a verismo musical as well as a traditional book musical. We think it is essential for modern musical theatre singers to be able to belt as well as to sing lyrically (male as well as female voices). For more information about changing voice quality see Chapter 3 pp 23-4 and *Singing and The Actor*, Chapter 12. You will be capable of holding a part in choral writing and will memorise music easily.

Singer-actor jobs range across the style board from *Into the Woods* to *Les Misérables* to *Carousel* to *The Goodbye Girl* to *Phantom of the Opera* to *Rent* and so on. A singer-actor can be working at any of the levels of competence that we shall outline later in the chapter. You do not have to be in the West End to be in this category.

What you will need at the audition
1. Take song material that is appropriate for the audition you are attending. This shows that you are familiar with the repertoire and understand the genre you are working in. Some musical theatre auditions are very specific; if the brief says to take Sondheim, take Sondheim. If the brief says bring a pop song, do not take Rodgers and Hammerstein. In addition you should have in your repertoire songs of different types: ballad, uptempo, comedy, point or patter number, a dramatic scene, and at least one pop number if you are intending to go up for pop musicals. These show your versatility as a performer through the medium of song.
2. You must have the ability to sing in a vocal style that is appropriate for the musical you are auditioning for. For instance, if you are auditioning for *A Little Night Music* and sing in a pop-belt style (that might be more suitable for, say, *Grease*), that would not be appropriate.
3. You need to be able to demonstrate vocal skill of a high quality: control of the instrument, good range and that special quality – vocal presence. You must show that you can hold an audience's attention both physically and vocally through the medium of song.

6. Booth-singers

This is a relatively small category because the nature of the work means that jobs are few and the turnover low. Often booth singers will maintain their job for several successive runs. Except in a show like *A Chorus Line* in which the dancers do appear on stage for the first scene and then work in the booth for the rest of the show, the singers are heard and not seen. Shows that require singers in the booth are always very physical; booth singers are there to swell the sound and boost it while those on stage are doing complex dance routines. You will be vocally skilled (possibly classically trained) with excellent music reading skills and a solid background in ensemble singing. This is the kind of work that suits session singers. Often the job will be just one strand of your professional life. You must have a reliable vocal technique and also be self-reliant as a musician. You will probably be singing your part alone or, at the most, with one other person. The fact that the rest of the cast is also singing your part on stage is quite irrelevant; you cannot rely on them. Booth singing will suit you if you like security and are not easily bored. Shows using booth singers include *Starlight Express, Grease, Cats, Pirates of Penzance* (Broadway version) and *A Chorus Line*.

What you will need at the audition
1. You must show that you have received a thorough training as a singer and musician, and that you can sing in the style appropriate to the musical.
2. Your range will be important; if you cannot cover easily the extremes of the writing then you will not be right for the job. For instance if you are singing the soprano line, you will probably be producing high C's every night.
3. You will need to demonstrate that you can follow the conductor and deal with changes of tempo and style when the show requires it.

Level of competence 2: your work arena

Many actors doing the round of musicals auditions do not know their own level of competence. If you don't know, how can you expect the panel to know? It is not a good idea to wait for a panel to tell you anything, least of all, where you are. In this section we are asking you to assess your current professional level. Make sure you look at the work categories below and answer them accurately. Remember that you can be in any of the singer categories described above and work in a variety of professional situations. If you are training for the profession, that is a category in itself. Here are the main situations where an actor finds work:
• Student: training full or part-time for the profession
• Fringe: ensemble/cover, named part, and lead
• Touring: ensemble, ensemble/cover, named part, lead and swing
• West End: ensemble, ensemble/cover, named part, lead and swing
The role of a swing in a production is almost a job category in itself. Large scale West End productions will always have at least one swing, and touring productions may have them as well, depending on the projected injury rate of the show.

The swing

You can work as a swing under any of the job categories we described above (singer-actor, singer-dancer and so on). You will need to be a good all-rounder within your genre to be a successful and happy swing. Many swings in fact cross the categories, hence they are ideal for the job they do. You will learn music and the details of staging quickly and probably find this quite instinctive. You will enjoy the challenge of doing different things in the same week, sometimes in the same show. You will need a good vocal range and the ability to change vocal characterisation and voice quality with ease.

Where are you now?

Now we are coming to the most important part of this process of self-examination: assessing your level. Beware of assessing your level from your last contract. Being a professional is not about where you are doing your work; it's about *what* you do and how well you do it. Make a list of the singing auditions that you have attended over the last eighteen months. If you are training, include in-house assessments and auditions.

- Decide which job category fits each audition. You might find that you are going for several different types of job.
- Make a list of the skills you would need to do each job: acting, physical, vocal, musical, and special skills.
- Assess your own skills levels as they are right now: acting, physical, vocal, musical, and special skills.
- Do your skills match with the jobs you are auditioning for? If not, in which areas do you need further or new training? And to what level?
- Are you are comfortable working at your current level? If the answer is 'no' you can now use the information given under the heading 'your level of competence' to work out what it is you need to move on. Then discuss with your agent, teacher, vocal coach or trusted colleague, how realistic is your aim. If the answer is yes, do not let anyone persuade you that you should be doing something else!

This process of assessment will enable you to give the clear picture that we have talked about as being essential for the panel to place you in auditions. It is not about pigeon-holing; it is perfectly possible for an actor to belong to more than one category, provided he or she has the requisite skills. We are going to do a similar process with your principal tool for the singing audition – your voice.

Chapter 3

Your Voice

Many actors do not know their singing voice very well and describe it as being deficient in some way. 'My voice only goes up to C' (or whatever note). Or, 'I don't have a belt voice'; 'my voice cracks', and so on. This is focusing on what your voice *is* rather than what it *does*. As soon as you do this you limit yourself: your voice is an instrument, capable of producing a wide range of notes and a variety of different voice qualities. In order to sing successfully in the theatre you need to be able to do everything that you do with your voice in spoken text, but using the medium of song. You need to be able to express both minute nuances of psychological shifts as well as broad sweeps of emotion. In addition, sung text demands that you deliver the words on certain pitches and within a rhythmic structure (the latter being akin to speaking in verse). This presents its own problems when you also want to convey the text intelligibly. These are what we consider to be the minimum requirements for good singing in the theatre:

1. To sing on pitch and in tune (these are not necessarily the same).
2. To know and manage your vocal range.
3. To have dynamic control: that is the ability to sing softly, loudly and all the gradations in-between.
4. To have a healthy voice production that will enable you to survive a run of performances because you are using your voice efficiently.
5. The ability to change voice quality: to vary it according to the style of song you are singing, or to match the psychological changes your character is experiencing during the course of the song.

Notice that we are not asking you to make a particular type of sound. There is no such thing as a 'singing voice'; there are just voices. Good singing is a skill that can be learned. You can find out how by working with a good teacher or by reading *Singing and The Actor*[1], a technical handbook for singers in the theatre. For now let's assume that you have addressed your training, and look at how to assess your vocal skills for the purposes of auditioning.

---

[1]*Singing and The Actor*, Kayes, A&C Black, January 2000

Pitching and tuning

We hope it is obvious that if you are having difficulty pitching notes you should not be presenting yourself for singing auditions. Pitching can be learned but for some people it can take a little time. Use the siren (see page 21) to ensure that you are on pitch any time that you are learning new music, especially in an audition situation. Similarly, if you are being asked in audition to demonstrate your range and are approaching either a very high or low note, siren it first to get your voice into position before you sing out. This will show to the panel that you know what you are doing with your voice. If you can siren the note on pitch then you know it is in your range and that you will be able to sing it.

Some singers have tuning issues that are not to do with the pitch itself. Even if you have a good voice and know how to put a song over, you may well be written off if you sing 'out of tune'. You may be making the right pitch with your vocal folds but the sound that comes out is flat or sharp. Here are a number of reasons why people have problems with their tuning:

1. Lack of resonance. The pitch is right but there are not enough harmonics (the 'family' of notes we hear around the main pitch) to make the note sound 'true'. This sometimes happens with singers who send air down their nose, because the nasal cavity damps down the resonances. Other times it can happen because the voice is insufficiently anchored[2] and therefore the singer cannot access full resonance.
2. Singing flat. This often happens with singers who force their larynx down with the back of the tongue, or who sing with a low larynx generally, believing that it is the way to make a 'big sound'.
3. Singing sharp. Singers who drive breath commonly sing sharp. The tiny vocal folds that make the sound are being asked to work too hard to resist the breath and so the pitch is forced up.

Many people talk about singing 'flat' or 'sharp' without knowing what it really means, so check things out for yourself if someone has said this about or to you. All of these issues can be sorted out with the help of a good teacher or vocal coach.

Assessing your range

We assess people's range by using the Siren exercise. The siren is described in detail in *Singing and The Actor*. It is important when

---

[2] For a definition of Anchoring see *Singing and The Actor*

looking at your range not to get confused by changes in voice quality. For instance, an actress who sings mainly in her chest voice might well think her singing range very limited but be able to get much higher using the siren. The siren therefore is an indication of your *actual* range. A good singer will usually have a three-octave range in their siren but will not necessarily sing all those notes in public. By using the siren, you will both develop and become accustomed to your full range. You cannot really determine your *working* range until you have done this.

Using the siren to determine actual range

1. Begin by putting your tongue and palate together in the 'NG' position as in the word 'sing'. Your tongue should be raised at the back and spread at the sides so that it is touching the upper back molars.
2. Start to make very small whining or mewing sounds with your tongue and palate still in this position. The sound must be very quiet and will be coming down your nose. You will need very little breath.
3. Now begin to make a larger excursion with your siren: try a pitch-glide in larger and larger loops that start and end with the same pitch. Remember to keep the sound quiet and small.
4. Finally, make the siren from the bottom to the top of your vocal range. The sound is similar to that of a child who is providing the sound effects for an American-style fire or police siren.

The top and bottom notes of your siren give you the extent of your vocal range. If your siren is less than two octaves you need to do some more work on your technique and on the siren exercise itself. It is normal for the siren to feel more difficult at certain points in your range (usually at the top and very bottom). It is also common for your voice to 'crack' or even to disappear at certain points in your range. The crack indicates that you have changed into another voice quality, not that you have necessarily reached the top of your range. If your voice disappears for a note or two and then reappears, this usually means that you have constricted and closed off inside the larynx.

If you can perform the siren from the top to the bottom of your range with no cracks and breaks, then you have management of your vocal range. You can work the siren in octave exercises with a piano or keyboard, as well as a noise exercise. You can also use the siren to learn songs by singing all the notes to 'NG' in the sirening position. The siren is a great way to improve the accuracy of your pitching and a very quick way to see if a song is in the right range for you.

Working range

Your working range is what you put down on your CV. Probably it will be somewhat less than your actual range because you will need to be able to produce the extremes reliably for eight shows a week. As a guide, we would expect a working singer to have two octaves of working range. You can expect to have to warm up and maintain your voice in its working range. Please note that your range is not defined by calling yourself soprano or mezzo, tenor or baritone; these refer to *types* of voice and are not necessarily range-specific. We will be looking at voice types and their comfort zone in Chapter 4.

Dynamic control

Are you in charge of the volume control of your voice? Some singers with otherwise good voices tend to produce their sound at the same dynamic level, no matter what. This limits their ability to interpret both the text and the music. It is also a disadvantage in ensemble singing where you need to be able to blend with the other singers. A singer without good dynamic control is ultimately inflexible as a performer. Some singers have difficulty controlling their dynamic level when moving across the range: they get louder as they go higher, simply because high notes require a greater input of effort. Conversely the same singers may well find that their voices disappear at the bottom of the range, because they do not know how to boost the volume level of their lowest notes. (High notes are heard as louder than low notes by the human ear.) Another type of singer has two sound levels: loud and brassy, or soft and breathy. They cannot produce anything in-between. Difficulties with dynamic control might also be a result of changing voice quality; there is, for instance, no such thing as quiet belting. Conversely a falsetto quality may be breathy and may not project well. You, not your voice, need to be in charge of your dynamic levels. Check that you can grade your dynamic levels over the majority of your vocal range.

Healthy voice

The health of your voice is of key importance for you, your agent and any company that you work for. You want to be able to rely on your voice for eight shows a week, perhaps over an entire year. What are the factors that might indicate that your voice is unhealthy?
1. Does your voice tire easily (e.g. after a lesson or during rehearsals)?
   Distinguish between the sensations of ache and scratch. Ache may be a normal response to newly worked muscles, although it should

never be prolonged or recurrent. Scratch means you are overworking, while soreness may indicate either that you have overworked or are ill.
2. Does it take you a long time to get your voice warmed up? Five to ten minutes is a good guideline.
3. Does your voice cut out on you a lot when you are not expecting it?
4. Is your voice *always* breathy or husky? (You may like the sound but it is not good for you!) Or are you constantly clearing your throat?
5. Does your speaking voice sound strange after you have been singing?

Any of these factors might mean that you are not using your voice efficiently. Perhaps your voice has become damaged due to poor use, or perhaps there is something physiologically wrong. If in doubt, seek advice from a Voice Clinic. The Voice Clinic staff can advise you on whether your problem can be helped by training, therapy, medication or surgery. It is not a good idea to go for auditions if you are having a voice problem: companies like performers who are reliable.

Changing voice quality

At this point we are not considering how your voice sounds habitually or 'naturally'. Singing and speaking in any case are learned behaviours, and there are all kinds of reasons why we sing or speak in a particular way. All voices can sing in any quality – all healthy voices can belt and can produce an operatic sound. It is the singer who makes the choice to do one or the other. This means that you can characterise your voice for different roles as well as for different styles of musical, and this makes you eminently more employable. These are the voice qualities described in *Singing and The Actor*[3]:
1. **Speech quality.** This is used for the musical theatre equivalent of operatic recitative. It is needed for narrative, direct communication, for patter songs and point numbers, and also for the verse sections of many songs. Speech quality is for those moments when you are not in song mode but have notes to sing. It is essential for the verismo musicals and anything through-composed, i.e. with no spoken text at all.
2. **Falsetto quality.** Produced by both male and female voices, this quality is needed for moments of reflection, intimacy, uncertainty and vulnerability. Falsetto quality does not project well without

[3]*Singing and The Actor*, Chapter 12

amplification in a large space but is otherwise used in all genres of musical theatre.

3. **Cry quality**. This is the warm and approachable sound needed for much ballad singing. It is characterised by vibrato (preferably not excessive) and sweetness of tone. Cry quality is a must for the romantic roles in book musicals, though it is not limited to these.

4. **Twang quality**. Twang enables any voice to carry well and is therefore invaluable in theatre singing. It is part of the vocal set-up for many styles of modern musical. Twang introduces 'edge' or brilliance to the tone. Twang is also used for character voices.

5. **Opera quality**. Certain roles in musical theatre require an operatic sound. Increasingly, some opera companies, such as D'Oyly Carte and Music Theatre London, are casting actor-singers in some of their productions. If you want to apply for these roles, you will need a more operatic set-up.

6. **Belt quality**. Belting is prevalent in the West End and on Broadway and is part of the contemporary musical theatre sound. You will need it for pop musicals, many concept musicals and for the verismo musicals. In the traditional book musicals it is often the character roles that require a belt quality. A versatile singer needs to be able to belt as well as to sing 'legit' (cry quality).

How familiar are you with these voice qualities and their use in current musical theatre? Even if the terminology is unfamiliar, do you recognise the territory? Theatre singing is not just concerned with the voice beautiful, and it is important for you to understand the vocal style implications of different types of musical.

When assessing your suitability for an audition, you will need to know whether or not you can sing in an appropriate style. This applies to any singer at any level; the important thing is to *know your genre*. We will talk much more about the style implications of different types of musical in Chapter 6.

Chapter 4

Casting Your Voice

You might be wondering at this stage what is your voice: are you a soprano or mezzo-soprano, baritone or tenor? If so, what do these terms really mean and how much do they tell about your voice? Is there a way of categorising voices? (Is there a way of categorising actors?)

At the simplest level – that of range and what we have defined as 'comfort zone' – the traditional categories (e.g. soprano and tenor) describe where a voice sits most comfortably in its range. However, there is more to a voice than the range of notes it can cover, and this is where things become both more complex and subjective. Here are some words that you might use to describe differences between two singers who are categorised as having the same voice type: Darker or brighter, covered or ringing, heavier or lighter, dramatic, lyric or young, bigger or smaller, thicker or thinner, warm or edgy, and so on

Assessing whether or not you like to sing in the soprano or mezzo-soprano range is relatively easy. Working out a useful way of describing your voice in more detail is not. Some of your vocal characteristics will be due to your muscular patterning and/or your training. By keeping an open mind about your voice and exploring all the qualities it can make, you will find that you are more versatile than you thought.

Physical factors

Firstly, every voice is unique, just as you are unique. The Three Tenors are all tenors, but each of them sounds distinct from the other. Some of these differences arise perhaps from doing something different mechanically to make their individual sound, but mostly they are due to differences in size of the physical frame and the voice itself. What we are concerned with here are characteristics that are 'natural' to your voice because of your physical characteristics. There are two main factors that will affect your personal vocal quality: the size of the vocal tract (the tube of your instrument) and the length and thickness of your vocal folds. A singer or actor with a big voice (wide core or thick sound) will almost certainly have thick or large vocal folds. If the vocal folds are also long, the singer is likely to be a lower voice. Short thin or small vocal folds are usually found on the voices of sopranos and tenors. The length and width of the vocal tract is also a consideration. When we talk about the vocal tract this includes the dimensions of the mouth and nasal cavity. A Pavarotti-like tenor will probably have a wide, short neck. A soprano with a big (dramatic) voice might well have a wide neck and large mouth cavity. A long vocal tract will result in a deeper, richer sound, and so on. You need to understand the limits of your voice as well as its versatility, which is why we have included this information in this section.

Singers who try to emulate the size of someone else's voice run into difficulties: you cannot sing like a Valjean if your voice is really a light baritone, and you will find it difficult to sing in the lyric Disney heroine style (such as Belle) if your voice is a weighty mezzo-soprano. Similarly sopranos who belt well will still not sound like Tina Turner or Cher: their sound will be thinner and smaller. And a natural tenor will end up pushing his voice if he tries to sing a heavy role such as Sweeney Todd.

In order to understand your voice type, you need to find your 'comfort zone'.

Comfort zone

You will remember that in the previous chapter we talked about full range and working range. Working range was smaller than the full range; your comfort zone will be smaller still. Your comfort zone is not just where singing feels easiest; it is also where your voice is most efficient, works best and shows to its best advantage. It is one indicator of your voice type. Your comfort zone may vary depending on which voice quality you are using, but in general it is where your voice sounds and feels easiest, and comes out without pushing. One female singer we worked with had an idea that her comfort zone was from low G to the E above middle C (the classic 'chest' range). After working the siren and giving herself permission to access the higher part her range, she discovered that her voice worked easiest from the F above middle C to the F above that, a classic soprano comfort zone. Without the experience of accessing her upper range, she had believed that as she could push the low notes that this was the area where her voice worked best.

In terms of choosing material, the *tessitura* of a song is defined by where the bulk of the song sits in terms of pitch. A song usually sits around a range of five or six notes, with odd phrases extending higher or lower. If these pitches are in your vocal comfort zone, this indicates that the song is in a good key for you.

The range you can expect from your voice category

Here are our guidelines for the expected working range of each of the voice categories.

Soprano

Working range   Comfort zone

Sopranos with smaller voices should not worry if the sound is much smaller at the very top than lower down in the range. High notes carry better than low notes and you are not singing dramatic opera. Mostly these top notes will be used in the chorus, but they have to be reliable because you will be producing them for eight shows a week. A typical example would be the ensemble in *Beauty and the Beast*. Leading roles for soprano include Laurie in *Oklahoma!*, Amalia in *She Loves Me* and Cosette in *Les Misérables*.

Belt begins at B/C above middle C and goes on up to F or beyond. Sopranos need to have good speech quality these days and should be able to take it up to at least G or A above middle C.

Mezzo-soprano

Working range   Comfort zone

Your voice should be strong and you should feel comfortable singing below the stave. However, if your voice stops at B or C above middle C then you are really limiting your chance of work. The role of Nettie in *Carousel* requires a good strong high G and is sung by a mezzo-soprano. A more contemporary example would be Florence in *Chess*.

Belt begins around F/G above middle C and should go on to the C or D above. Your belt voice will be darker and thicker than that of a soprano.

Contralto

Working range   Comfort zone

True contralto voices are very rare. If you sing alto in the choir, it doesn't make you a contralto. However, there is a current trend in musical theatre in writing lower for the female voice. An example might be Spider Woman in *The Kiss of The Spider Woman*, who sings repeated low C#'s (below middle C) in the title song of the show. Gillyanne worked with one young woman who could sing this number easily, and she also had a good top A. She might well be classed as a contralto voice. Music is sometimes written in the contralto range to denote age. A good example would be the song 'Liaisons' from *A Little Night Music* where the character is venerably aged and, in fact, dies before the play is concluded. The range for this song is D below middle C to the F# above. It is likely that if you ever see a role advertised for contralto, it will be for an older character.

(It is worth mentioning here that there is also a trend in pop music for writing low in the female voice. Cher is a notable example as is Britney Spears. Bear in mind however, that these singers enjoy the benefit of a sound production team when they perform live and that the genre or popular music today owes as much to the work of skilled production team as to the voice of the performer.)

Your comfort zone will usually be between low F and the G above middle C. Beware! This is also the territory of heavy smokers; vocal folds damaged by smoking can often no longer stretch for the upper range.

Tenor

Working range   Comfort zone

There are different types of tenors, and some do not sing as high as others but are still tenors. Let's start by defining a tenor as a male voice that is happy to sing above the stave (reading music in the treble) without having to use his falsetto voice. Some tenors can go up to high B but stop there; others can go on up to high D in full voice. The lighter voiced tenors will usually be able to go down to low A, so long as they do not have to stay down there. A bigger voiced tenor might well have quite powerful bottom notes that sound not unlike a baritone but will still not really go beyond low A or G. A key feature of a tenor voice that is working is that it seems to 'kick into gear' around the upper D or E, whereas a baritone has to work harder at this point in his range. All tenors can belt (provided they learn how) and rock tenors *must* be able to belt. You cannot do the role of Judas in *Jesus Christ Superstar* or Trumper in *Chess* unless you have a good strong belt.

Belt begins at high A/B and carries on upwards.

Baritone

Working range   Comfort zone

The average male singing voice falls into the baritone category. The notes given for the top of the working range should be in full voice, not falsetto. You do have these notes if you are a baritone, although they are probably not in your comfort zone: you will have to work to get them. Examples of baritone roles include Javert in *Les Misérables* (he has to sing F#s) and Stine in *City of Angels*. Javert would not be suitable for a tenor because the character is too dark; Stine is a leading man with a twist (certainly not always likeable); he is neither a romantic nor an epic hero and is so more suited to a baritone voice.

Belt begins at F#/high G and carries on upwards (above middle C). We have found that many baritones can extend their range by accessing belt quality. Sometimes this is the only way you can get a high A if you are a heavy voiced baritone.

Bass

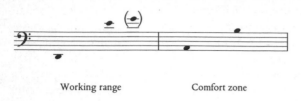

Working range   Comfort zone

The bass voice is simply a big voice with a large range. Many bass voices can go as high as baritones or even tenors, but they do not sit comfortably there, and the main characteristic of their sound will be warmth, richness and darkness. In musical theatre, bass voices tend to be the older characters: a bass voice denotes gravitas. It might also denote power or a sinister quality. Musical theatre writing is getting higher and higher for the male voice at the moment, so if you really are a bass, make sure that you work the top of your range so that you are employable during your early years as a performer. Roles for the bass voice might be Caiaphas in *Jesus Christ Superstar* (low D's) and Max in *Sunset Boulevard* (high Gb's). A category called bass-baritone also exists denoting a baritone range with an extra dark tone.

Belt range for bass begins at D/E above middle C and carries on upwards.

Some of the notes we have given for your expected range might be outside your comfort zone. That's OK; it just means that you need to work to develop your range. What you want to avoid is putting your voice into a different category than it really is, just because you have not found your true working range. Usually people feel limited by the upper part of their range, but not always. Here are three examples of from Gillyanne's studio of singers who were confused about their voice type.

1. SC, a young dancer-singer came for lessons concerned that she could only reach the E a tenth above middle C; her voice 'did not seem to go any higher'. On her CV she had defined herself as a mezzo-soprano, but actually the bottom of her voice was neither strong nor the range extensive. The sound that she made in the middle and bottom of her range was simply not thick enough to class her as a mezzo-soprano. At an audition, the panel might well be disappointed when she started to sing. Really she was a soprano who just hadn't found her top notes. We worked to develop the top of her range and found music to suit her casting type for lyric ballads and for pop belt numbers. (Celine Dion provides good soprano belt material.) In extending her range

down to low G and up to top B she became more viable for a wider range of castings.

2. SF, an actor-singer came for lessons singing a lot of low repertoire. Actually her voice was really soprano and what we would define as a big voice with the potential to be dramatic. Big voices take a long time to develop and so the singer had been given a lot of songs that were not really suitable for her and could only really sing in 'chest voice'. When she went up in the range, there was a noticeable difference between her bottom and middle range. This difference is really to do with voice quality and not voice type; this singer was not a mezzo. A further difficulty with this actress was that, in terms of casting, she was likely to get character or strong best friend types roles. We began by finding the whole working range, and we set it in order. This enabled me to find where her voice worked best and then to find the right repertoire that could be performed in a voice quality to suit her casting category. We found songs that had strength, solidity and humour in them where she was able to use her speech quality and belt but could stay within her higher comfort zone, e.g. *'What More Do I Need?'* (*Marry Me A Little*) and *'Funny'* (*Funny Girl*).

3. I worked with an actor (CO) in his twenties at a drama school. This man was tall with quite a large frame. He really enjoyed listening to the pop and soul repertoire and came to college singing in high speech quality and falsetto. With work we discovered that his voice was really bass baritone. He was still able to access the falsetto range, but he now also had vocal depth to match his dramatic personality. He went on to sing the role of Sweeney Todd in a college production and found that he could still sing the soul repertoire he liked using the female key an octave lower. This is a useful ploy for singing pop repertoire if you are a bass.

To summarise, although a soprano and a mezzo-soprano often have a similar range, the soprano will get going at D a ninth above middle C, whereas the mezzo-soprano will be stronger and more vibrant in the lower and middle notes. Likewise, a tenor will kick into gear around E above middle C, whereas a baritone will be stronger and more vibrant on the middle notes. All of this is assuming that your voice is well set up and that you have worked your range.

Singing in falsetto

There is a great deal of confusion about what is and isn't falsetto. We believe *falsetto quality* in musical theatre is not confined to the upper

ranges of men's voices; women as well as men can make this type of
falsetto. This sound may be somewhat breathy and can be produced
with more or less 'core' over the whole range. This is not to be
confused with the 'crack' that may happen at the upper end of a
man's range. While a man can access falsetto quality most easily at
this point, in fact this crack is merely another gear change in the
voice, and it can be managed in any voice quality. We have had male
singers in our studio who can produce a rock scream up to soprano
top C! However, the purpose of this book is not to offer a definition
of falsetto. Many musical theatre pieces now demand that men can
sing falsetto, so we recommend that you learn to access it and use it
efficiently. Typical examples of songs requiring falsetto are the '*Sun
and Moon Duet*' from *Miss Saigon* and '*Those Magic Changes*' from
Grease.

What if my face doesn't fit my voice?

There is an interesting point to be made here about the 'fach' system
used for classical singers. 'Fach' is a German word meaning work or
speciality. It is a detailed system, giving a lot more information about
singers' voices than just the ranges. By using the system, singers can
avoid putting themselves into the position of taking on roles that are
unsuitable for them. It also enables those who are employing them to
call the right type of voice to audition for productions. Like actors,
classical singers may change fach as their careers develop. You can see
the parallel with the theatrical tradition of casting types. However,
there is a major difference in that in the theatre we cast by physical
and dramatic type first and voice second, even in musicals. So what
happens if your voice doesn't fit your face? We suggest that you be
guided by your casting type *first*. Audiences will often accept a
performer who is the right physical type in a role more easily than if
he/she has a good voice but isn't convincing in the role. You may be
naturally a wonderful high soprano, but if you look like a character
actress and are cast in those roles as an actress you should find songs
for your voice type that show your ability as a character actress. This
is not difficult to do, and we will be discussing it when we look at
how to choose songs that suit you.

Here is an idea of the type of voice and song that may be likely to
match with the common casting categories. We cannot give you hard
and fast rules about this; musicals are enormously varied in their
writing for voices and type of song.

Young female lead

She will often sing ballads and needs to be able to sing lyrically. She is more likely to be a soprano (e.g. Laurie in *Oklahoma!*, Amalia in *She Loves Me*, Belle in *Beauty and the Beast*, and Johanna in *Sweeney Todd*).

Young female character

She will do the funny quirky numbers (e.g. Ado Annie in *Oklahoma!*, Carrie in *Carousel*, Martha in *The Secret Garden*, Petra in *A Little Night Music*, and Ilona in *She Loves Me*). She is more likely to be a mezzo-soprano, but a soprano can do these roles provided that she can use speech quality and has good belt. Point and patter numbers are the mainstay; ballads are less likely.

Young male lead

He will often sing the romantic ballad. Nowadays he is most often a high baritone or a tenor (e.g. Curly in *Oklahoma!*, Marius in *Les Misérables*, and Cinderella's Prince in *Into the Woods*).

Young male character

Roles include Benoit in *Martin Guerre* and Will Parker in *Oklahoma!* He is usually tenor or light baritone and is more likely to sing point or patter numbers than ballads.

Leading lady

She will sing strong dramatic numbers, sometimes also romantic. Roles include Fosca in *Passion*, Paula in *The Goodbye Girl*, Kim in *Miss Saigon* (leading lady for young performer) Charity in *Sweet Charity*, Mabel in *Mack and Mabel*, and Spider Woman in *The Kiss of the Spider Woman*. She is most likely to be a mezzo-soprano or soprano with a big dramatic voice. A strong belt may be needed, especially nowadays. She may well sing ballads that include belt as well as contrasting uptempo numbers. It is likely that she will have to sing duets and trios, so she must have good musical skills. She must be versatile vocally and should be a very strong singer.

Leading man

Roles include Jean Valjean in *Les Misérables*, Martin Guerre in the title role, Chris in *Miss Saigon*, Mack Sennett in *Mack and Mabel*, the baker in *The Baker's Wife*, Sweeney Todd in the title role, George in *Sunday In The Park With George*, and Billie Bigelow in *Carousel*. He must be a performer with a strong dramatic presence. Interestingly a baritone can sing most leading man roles provided that he has good top notes.

Jean Valjean, however is for dramatic tenor, as is Chris, and Sweeney Todd requires a dark baritone or bass voice. Don't forget that there are second leads as well, who must be equally strong singers. If the lead is a baritone, the second lead might well be a tenor and vice versa. Expect to sing dramatic ballads, duets and trios as well as faster numbers.

Female character
Roles include Nettie in *Carousel*, Old Woman in *Candide*, Madame Thenardier in *Les Misérables*, Shenzie in *The Lion King*, and Mama Morton in *Chicago*. These roles are usually sung by a mezzo-soprano or soprano with good speech quality. In the classic book musicals a more operatic sound is often required, and in more contemporary works, belt voice. Expect to sing point numbers, true uptempi and some patter numbers.

Male character
Roles include Hakem in *Oklahoma!*, Herod in *Jesus Christ Superstar*, Mysterious Man in *Into the Woods*, Engineer in *Miss Saigon*, Fagin in *Oliver* (character lead role), and Scar in *The Lion King*. He is often a tenor, but most roles could be sung by a high baritone. Lyric singing is not required. Point and patter numbers are the mainstays of material.

You will want to refer to this list again when you have done the work we suggest in the following chapter. If you are concerned that your face doesn't fit your voice, it really is a matter of being creative about your audition portfolio. If you are a character actress, find ballads that have a twist to them or a comic content, rather than straight romance.

In audition workshops and in private classes we always ask actors to define their casting category. While we recognise that actors do not like to be pigeonholed, the casting categories are useful in that they describe the area where you have worked or are likely to work the most. We then ask the actors if they think their voice fits their casting category.

Here are two examples of responses we got at workshops where we asked actors to describe their singing voice and then their casting category.

JR was an actress with a high soprano voice; she was very able in the upper range and had an excellent belt voice. She could sing the romantic juvenile leads but knew that she would never be cast in those roles because of her physical type. We found a wide range of songs for her that would enable her strengths as a character actress to show. We avoided straight romantic ballads and replaced them with numbers like '*Dear Friend*' from *She Loves Me* (comedy with pathos), '*Child of Newgate*' from *Moll Flanders* (a strong, dramatic ballad with good belt notes in it), and we used comic soprano songs such as '*Vanilla Ice Cream*' to show off her top notes. Her uptempo numbers included songs like '*I Can Cook Too*' from *On the Town* and '*Happily Ever After*' from *Once Upon a Mattress* showing her strong narrative and comic skills. Although she could actually sing them very well, we avoided leading lady songs such as '*Don't Rain on My Parade*' from *Funny Girl* because they would give a confusing message to the audition panel.

RL was an actor with a powerful baritone voice with the potential to be very dramatic. In looks he was quite boyish and slightly quirky and had made the mistake of doing light comedy and vaudeville type numbers that did not suit his voice. He felt that he wasn't getting recalls because he could not sing the mainstream tenor numbers that he felt the panel wanted to hear. We felt that this was potentially the voice of a leading man with the physique of a character actor. We helped him develop his belt voice so that he could sing a top A if needed, and encouraged him to develop the stronger and slightly more sinister sides of his character. Soon after he was cast in a West End musical.

A good singing teacher or vocal coach will help you to find out your voice type and explore repertoire so that you can find material that suits you. Use the information you have gathered from this chapter to help them and yourself. This brings us nicely to the topic of our next chapter: how to choose material that suits *you*.

Chapter 5

What Makes You Special?

Gillyanne. A while ago I was teaching an actress who had not really worked in the profession since drama college. She had a good voice and worked hard with me to learn the voice qualities required for the different styles of musical theatre singing. Her belt voice was excellent, and she also had a lovely lyric soprano voice. People were always impressed with her singing at auditions, but somehow she never got the job. She rang me in great excitement one day, asking if she could have a lesson in a couple of days' time. She had been called to audition for a role in a West End show and wanted some coaching. She told me she had found just the right song for the audition; perfect for the role she was auditioning for, and she hoped that the panel would be 'really impressed' with it. She had got hold of the music and needed to learn the song with me. I wondered, after I had put the phone down, why this actress was so intent on learning a new song for the audition; she had plenty of suitable material in her portfolio that was well prepared and up to performance standard.

Later, when we talked about this, I realised that she had been facing the wrong way in thinking about the audition. By thinking about what the panel might want to hear and about what might persuade them that she would be right for the role, she had left herself out of the equation. The songs that are right for an audition are the songs that are *right for you*. Ideally you only want to learn a new song for an audition when you have already received a call back and have been asked to learn something new (usually a song from the show). While we believe it is possible to learn new material fast to performance standard, on the whole it is best avoided. The key point about this story is that you cannot prepare for an audition if 'the boat is pointing the wrong way', i.e. at you and not moving away from you. If you are making all your choices as a performer from the panel's point of view (what do they want? what will they like?) you are likely to make choices that will sabotage your chances of doing a good job at the audition.

36

Making the most of you

Have you ever noticed two women wearing the same dress at a party? Did they both look good in it, but somehow different? What about when you see someone in an outfit that is clearly expensive but doesn't do anything for them? You want a song that will make the most of *you*. As an experienced audition pianist, Jeremy has often had to play the same piece for many different people. The unsuccessful performances are not always due to poor preparation. The performer may have chosen a song or a character that is outside what we call their Falling-Off-A-Log area. Your *FOAL* area is something that you do so instinctively that you may not even realise you are good at it, or discount your ability completely, because you don't have to 'try'. Sometimes you can only recognise your own *FOAL* area when you see someone else doing the same repertoire. Perhaps they don't understand how to make it work, yet to you it seems obvious. When a song is in your *FOAL* area, you will already have an understanding on a deep level of what the situation means to the character, so you have a head-start in your preparation. You are then working from a position of authority. Witnessing someone working from their own *FOAL* area is unmistakable: there is an extra depth of understanding that is authentic and truthful. Here is a real- life example of what we mean in practice by Falling-Off-A-Log.

A soprano working for an opera company performed three different roles. As the maid, driving the action with comic fizz, she could not excel: the framework of the character did not allow her to use the heights and depths of emotion that she was suited to. (The woman who had originally created the role of the maid in that production *had* been working in her *FOAL* area, and was able to show her abilities to their best advantage.) However, as the neurotic woman she was extremely accomplished, singing the music with a real understanding of the situation. As the heroine devastated by appalling news, she was dramatically and vocally superb and fully up to the emotional extremes of the role while staying within the framework of style. (Note that the original maid could not have excelled at the other two roles; they were outside her *FOAL* area.)

Working through this and the next three chapters gives you the information you need to build an audition portfolio. The songs you eventually narrow down from your original database will suit you, your voice, your personality and your casting. More than that, they will enable you to shine at what you do best.

Choosing songs from the inside out

There are different types of song – ballads, uptempo numbers and all their subcategories. There are also different styles of musical. There are different voice types and different casting categories. There are, literally, thousands of songs to choose from, even if we limit ourselves to musical theatre repertoire of the last fifty years. Most musicals and different styles of musical have several different types of song in them – it's part of the genre – you are never going to have a dearth of choice. So how on earth do you choose the music that is going to be right for you?

Begin with yourself. Do not choose a song to impress the panel, or because it suits the character you are not yet playing, or even because nobody else does it (though this can be advantageous). Choose songs that resonate with you and who you are: songs that are in your *FOAL* area. Based on the concept of choosing songs from the inside out, we have developed a process that can help you find out your *FOAL* area. We are looking at what you do to relax, what you do to unwind, and what holds your attention. Your hobbies and interests are self-serving, you don't normally keep up a hobby simply because you feel you 'ought to' or for the sake of your career. Your answers to the interview questions will reflect your areas of interest and agreement, and things that are meaningful to you.

The *FOAL* Process is in three stages. Stage I is the Interview, a process of gathering information about yourself. Stage II is a two-part analysis of the answers you have given that will reveal keywords and phrases. The two layers of analysis are 'Type' and 'Essence'. Stage III of the process shows you how to use the keywords and phrases to build a personal profile (Your Profile).

THE *FOAL* PROCESS

I. The Interview

Using the chart at the back of this book, fill in your answers to the following list of questions. You may not have answers to all of the questions, and some may be easier to answer than others. Note which ones you can give instant or multiple answers to, as this can be as important as your actual answers. Also write down any examples of things you hate in the list: your strong dislikes can give valuable information about the areas that have resonance for you. You may find it easier to do this with the help of a friend. Only after you have answered all the questions should you proceed with the analysis.

1. Who are your favourite stand-up comedians? Are there any you strongly dislike?
2. What are your favourite sitcoms or comedy programmes?
3. What are your favourite TV/radio dramas, named (e.g. *Inspector Morse*) or by genre (e.g. detective)?
4. What are your favourite soaps or long-running dramas? Are there any you hate?
5. What other types of programming do you like (e.g. documentaries, nature programmes, arts programmes, etc)?
6. What are your favourite films?
7. What are your favourite books?
8. Who are your favourite actors (male or female)? Are there any you strongly dislike?
9. What are your favourite theatre pieces, named (e.g. *King Lear*) or by genre (e.g. Shakespearean tragedies)?
10. What music do you like? Separate between active listening and background or mood-enhancing.
11. What are your hobbies, sports or physical activities? Are there any types you strongly dislike?

Answers at Stage I might look like this:

Stage I. The Interview	Stage IIa. Type	Stage IIb. Essence
1. Victoria Wood		
1. Eddie Izzard		
2. Dislike sitcoms		
3. Miss Marple Investigates		
3. Bob and Rose		
3. Dislike Cracker		
etc		

II. The Analysis

a. Type

The top layer of information identifies the genre from which an answer comes, and the general type within the genre. Describe each of your answers *in one phrase* (imagine talking to a friend who isn't familiar with them). We have given you some examples to start you off.

Comedians: stand-up train-of-thought, stand-up physical, stand-up joke telling, stand-up situation, comedy character

Sitcoms: domestic, relationship, surreal, character sketch, language-based

TV drama: contemporary, period, comedy-drama, gritty, crime, serial, children's, long-running sequential, science fiction

TV soaps: dramatic highs and lows, ordinary, down-to-earth, fast-moving storylines, slow build

Other TV: nature programmes, travel programmes, current affairs, documentary, historical, children's programming, informational, life-style, entertainment, chat show, game show

Books: thrillers, legal or courtroom, adventure, sci-fi, biography, romantic, classics, historical novels, non-fiction, self-development, New Age

Films: current, period, comedy, gritty, crime, children's, cartoons (animation), blockbusters, Bollywood

Actors: leading man, character, comedy actor, strong character

Theatre: naturalistic, fantastical, theatrical, conversational, modern, restoration

Music-type of listening: active (the music has your full attention); passive (background music to other tasks such as driving, at work, or socialising)

Type of music: classical orchestral, instrumental, vocal recital, vocal opera, choral, early music, world music, New Age, easy listening, jazz vocal, jazz instrumental, country, gospel, soul or blues, pop (anything from Motown and disco to garage and gangsta)

Hobbies: crafts (needlework, marquetry, pottery, DIY), visual (jigsaws, painting), visual competitive (computer games), physical competitive (football, tennis), physical non-competitive (yoga, aerobics), outdoor pursuits (canoeing, mountain biking, hiking), collecting (antiques, philately)

Here is our example with Stage IIa completed:

Stage I. The Interview	Stage IIa. Type	Stage IIb. Essence
1. Victoria Wood	Stand-up situation	
1. Eddie Izzard	Stand-up train-of-thought	
2. Dislike sitcoms	Situations with audience	
3. Miss Marple Investigates	Murder mystery	
3. Bob and Rose	Relationship drama	
3. Dislike Cracker	Crime drama	
etc		

b. Essence

Now describe to your friend the 'subtext' – the feel or flavour – of each example: warmth, style, approach, detail, power of drama, depth of characterisation, character type, emotional overtones. This becomes the second layer of analysis: the Essence.

Here are some example words:

Sarcastic, soft-edged, off-the-wall, slapstick, witty, creative, hardline, blue, political, satirical, bittersweet, romantic, subversive, epic, action, suspense, intelligent, philosophical, comic, cathartic, escapist, surreal, gritty, wide-angle, close detail, current, historical, people or buildings/land based, investigative, light-hearted, cheesy, basic, clever, outrageous, intricate, relationship, philosophical, spiritual, uplifting, depressing, life-changing, percipient, informative, exciting, gripping, calming, arousing, energised.

Here is our example with Stage IIb completed:

Stage I. The Interview	Stage IIa. Type	Stage IIb. Essence
1. Victoria Wood	Stand-up situation	Warm, domestic, witty
1. Eddie Izzard	Stand-up train-of-thought	Bizarre, surreal, witty
2. Dislike sitcoms	Situations with audience	Hate canned laughter, brainless
3. Miss Marple Investigates	Murder mystery	Period, quaint, detailed
3. Bob and Rose	Relationship drama	Warm, slightly controversial
3. Dislike Cracker	Crime drama	Too violent and gory
etc		

III. Your Profile

Take your list of words and look for trends: similarities and strong differences. Things that appear to be contradictory can be very useful in finding your *FOAL* area. This should shorten your list, and you can then précis what remains into five or six key phrases. It is important when analysing your answers that you don't look for trends until you have finished answering all the questions.

In our short example warm and witty, domestic and detailed appear, together with surreal, quaint and slightly controversial; gory and violent are not liked, together with the mindless aspect of 'being told when to laugh'. Therefore the *FOAL* Profile might read '**warm and witty but with a twist, detailed but not clinical (gory), independent**'.

Here are two examples of the *FOAL* Process in action.
NM, female, dancer-singer

Stage I. The Interview	Stage IIa. Type	Stage IIb. Essence
1. Lee Evans (instantly)	Stand-up physical, situation	Slapstick, creative
1. Ben Elton (later)	Stand-up joke telling, satire	Political, sarcastic, hard-line
2. Friends	Relationship	Warm, one-liners
3. No particular TV dramas		
4. Eastenders	Gritty drama	Dramatic highs and lows
4. Coronation Street	Domestic drama	Down-to-earth, slower developments
5. Nature programmes	Animals, not landscapes, close camera work	Community, relationship, details, behind the scenes
6. Muriel's Wedding	Human comedy-drama	Loner triumphing in adversity, optimism
7. A Child Called It	Relationship novel	Lonely child working through hard times
7. Love Is A Four Letter Word	Relationship novel	Lonely child working through hard times
7. Spanish & Latin American Culture (Learning Spanish)	Informational	Detail and community, stretching the imagination
7. 'Information' books	Informational	Detail and community, knowledge, interaction
7. Famous Five series – favourite character Anne	Children's drama serial	Anne was feminine, loved communicating, quite strong
8. No particular actors		

continued...

Stage I. The Interview	Stage IIa. Type	Stage IIb. Essence
9. *No particular theatre*		
10. *Latin Music, esp. Cuban*	*Background world*	*Energised and sunny*
10. *Albinoni Adagio*	*Classical instrumental, Baroque*	*Wistful*
10. *Tchaikowsky ballet music*	*Classical orchestral, Romantic*	*Romantic, music to move to, classic stories*
11. *Just bought first flat*	*Major event*	*Home and security*

List of key words

You can see that there are several strong trends in NM's answers.

From this list, we found the following key phrases:

Feminine, communication, strong, sunny, detailed, information, imagination, romantic but strong, lonely but not necessarily of her own volition, home and security.

Note that it was not necessary to provide an answer for every question. NM did not come up easily with responses to the film question, for example, because this was an area that she did not resonate with. Strong dislikes however *can* be included because they are usually significant. If you are not able to give answers quite quickly in a particular area then move on to another. If you are doing the Interview for someone else and they are not coming up with answers, be creative!

JT (male) is an actor-singer with strong dance skills. Using his answers to the Interview, we'll look more closely at how we arrive at the final key phrases in the analysis.

Additional information

Strong dislikes include physical exertion, although JT had had extensive training as a dancer. Other strong dislikes include: feeling removed, things with no context, formal language, slow moving plots It was interesting to note that, although Changing Rooms (Q.5) was a favourite, a similar programme where the room changes were valued by an estate agent did not appeal at all. In this case JT felt the interest was in watching the people interact, not in the monetary value of the changes.

Stage I. The Interview	Stage IIa. Type	Stage IIb. Essence
1. Victoria Wood	Stand-up situation	Warm, domestic, witty
1. Billy Connolly	Stand-up observational	Warm, spiky, grounded
1. Strong Dislike Roy 'Chubby' Brown	Stand-up joke telling	Crude
2. Friends	Relationship	Warm, one-liners
2. Gimme Gimme Gimme	Relationship	Grittier comedy, rude, one-liners, domestic
2. Round the Horne (radio)	Sketch/character	Witty, clever twists on words
3. This Life	Contemporary drama	Offbeat, edgy, unusual, unpredictable
3. Strong dislike	Period drama	Language not immediate, distancing
4. Eastenders	Gritty drama	Great highs and lows, fast-moving storylines
4. Dynasty	Glossy drama	Glossy, fast-moving, slightly exaggerated & tongue-in-cheek
4. Sunset Beach (short term)	Glossy drama	Fantasy, exaggerated, great for dipping into
4. Dislike Coronation Street Dallas	Domestic drama Glossy drama	Both have slower pace, build to the set-pieces are slower
5. The South Bank Show	Arts	Information & social comment, puts things in context
5. The Late Show	Discussion	Immediacy of conversation, and social comment

continued...

Stage I. The Interview	Stage IIa. Type	Stage IIb. Essence
5. Changing Rooms	Entertainment/lifestyle	Beyond reality, focus on people's lives and reactions as much as the decorating
5 Strong dislikes documentary, nature, & archaeology programmes		Not interested in what a fragment of a pot might look like. Prefers linking things with people, societal.
6. The Prime of Miss Jean Brodie	Relationship drama	Detailed, social comment, fine performances.
6. Beautiful Thing	Relationship drama	Well-crafted, warm
6. Singing in The Rain	Film Musical	Feel-good, well-crafted, a definitive. Film into stage musical
6. Funny Girl	Film Musical	Warm, funny, poignant. All four films chosen have also been stage plays.
7. Tales From the City	Novel, serial	Warm and acerbic, soap-like short scenes, every scene plays its part
7. Stephen Fry books (The Liar, The Hippopotamus)	Novel, comedy drama	Well-written, interesting use of language, witty
8. Judi Dench	Female lead	Multi-layered, solidity and truth, empathy
8. Ian McKellen	Male character	Skilled, integrated, suave
8. Robert Downey jr.	Male lead	Quirky, talented, danger
9. Swan Lake - Adventures in Motion Pictures	Ballet, classic myth with modern twist	Naturalistic and fantastical

continued...

Stage I. The Interview	Stage IIa. Type	Stage IIb. Essence
9. Rent	Contemporary musical, relationship	Theatricality and power
9. Blood Brothers	Contemporary musical	Domestic-social drama, vernacular
9. Jonathon Harvey plays – Out in The Open	Contemporary drama	Conversational, modern writing.
10. Listens both actively and passively (mostly active), R&B, Pop, They're Playing Our Song, Rent, Dreamgirls, Starting Here Starting Now, & various solo cabaret singers	Hardcore chart, R&B, torch songs, musical theatre	Much of the music listed here is in the form of songs with strong storylines, 'one-act play' songs, songs with emotion, good lyrics
11. Socialising	Pub and chat rather than club	Interaction with a view to talking

There are several distinct strands in JT's answers and more layers than merely 'warm and theatrical'. The warmth is offset by the spikiness and unpredictability, definitely not slushy. There is a pleasure in words, their use and context (he admitted to being fascinated by them). An appreciation of well structured and well written work runs throughout, together with an acknowledgement of 'the definitive', even if he did not like the result. Conversation and human interaction are very important, which means immediacy of communication is very strong. JT does not need things to be gentle, and is comfortable with the slightly grittier side of life, although the gritty end of his spectrum is usually linked with warmth to tone it down; we wouldn't say that Corialanus would be in his comfort zone! Note the inclusion of naturalistic *and* fantastical (his own suggestion). He is comfortable with things being complex, multi-layered and apparently contradictory.

From this information we can narrow it down to five or six phrases: warm and spiky, conversational and immediate, unusual and unpredictable, community and people, contextual, well written and well crafted. In choosing repertoire for his database, we would look particularly at the first three phrases.

The information from the *FOAL* Process can be used in many ways. (Jeremy has bought some very apt birthday presents for his brother using the key phrases in his Profile.) We will now show you how to use 'Your Profile' to build a database of songs that fit your *FOAL* area.

BUILDING YOUR DATABASE: GATHERING A LIST OF SONG TITLES

Having completed the *FOAL* Process, you should now have a list of keywords in your Profile. But how do you match your Profile with your repertoire? The analysis techniques in Stages IIa and IIb can also be applied to songs. To find the top layer of information (Type) in a favourite song, describe it in one word or phrase to a friend who does not know it. To reveal the subtext phrases in the second layer (Essence), look at the text, listen to the music, and imagine the staging that you would like to be part of. Then find key phrases to describe the feel of the song, or your impression of the character. For the moment, do not worry about whether you would be cast in the role, or even whether it was written for your gender. Look for material across the board, in and out of your casting and playing range. The aim is to build up a database of possible songs first and to do the categorising later. For this reason we have not yet talked about the different styles of musical or types of song; that comes in the next chapter. Just make a note of the songs that you think will suit you, even if they are not in the genre that you think of yourself performing in.

We'll use NM's Profile to look at possible repertoire for her personal database.

Feminine, communication, strong, sunny, detailed, information, imagination, romantic but strong, lonely but not necessarily of her own volition, home and security.

One of the songs she had chosen to bring was perfect for her: 'At Times Like This' from *Lucky Stiff*. The girl is lonely, and she is wistful but not wimpish. She is feminine and quite strong but a little sad, and she longs for someone to be with her forever. It is a romantic song, for someone portraying late teens, possibly early twenties. She knows that at times like this what you need is a dog (a faithful friend). NM tends to play kids or teenagers, and this song is a route to a slightly more mature character.

Other songs that came up for inclusion were:

'*Blame It on a Summer Night*' from *Rags*: in a strange land, explorative, looking forward to romance, sunny and positive.

'*Home*' from *Beauty and the Beast*: wistful, lonely, importance of home and security, strength.

'*Hold On*' from *The Secret Garden*: grounded and strong with warmth and optimism.

'*Cheer Up Charlie*' from *Charlie and The Chocolate Factory*: warmth, strength, family, encouraging optimism.

'*In Whatever Time We Have*' from *Children of Eden*: positive in adversity, strength, community.

'*Christmas Lullaby*' from *Songs For a New World*: feminine, romantic, strong.

'*Nice Work If You Can Get It*' (Gershwin): upbeat, wistful.

Here are song examples for JT.

JT's key phrases were:

Warm and spiky, conversational and immediate, unusual and unpredictable, community and people, contextual, well written and well crafted.

Suitable songs might be:

'*Empty Chairs At Empty Tables*' from *Les Misérables*: fellowship, working for a cause.

'*Bui-Doi*' from *Miss Saigon*: similar, with a wider mission of advocacy.

'*Another Day/Glory*' from *Rent*: spikey, direct, unpredictable.

'*If I Sing*' from *Closer Than Ever*: warm, family, well crafted.

'*Two People In Love*' from *Baby*: bringing the personal into a wider context.

'*Tell My Father*' from *The Civil War*: community and family, life values.

'*Good Thing Going*' from *Merrily We Roll Along*: assessing a personal or working relationship journey.

'*Our Time*' from *Merrily We Roll Along*: companionship, place in the community, warmth and hopefulness.

It's important that you start off your database with as many song titles as you can find. Over the years you will develop as a performer: your dramatic range may expand, your casting may change and you will get older. You will want to keep abreast of these changes by reviewing your personal database from time to time, so that it reflects your current skills and personality. Once your database is in place you can then use the information in the next chapter to sort the songs into Style categories.

Chapter 6

Know Your Genre!

Now you know how to choose material that suits you, and you have a database of possible audition songs. How will you know which song to take to which audition? In order to help you make the right choices we have assigned categories to types of musical, and to types of song. In order to ensure that you perform the song in an appropriate style we shall examine the hallmarks of different musical and vocal styles. The information in this chapter is quite detailed, but it will enable to you research your audition material yourself, rather than relying on someone else to do it for you in a singing lesson or coaching session.

There are all kinds of cues that we respond to when we listen to a song and the artist who is singing it. When we say that 'so-and-so has style' we tend to mean either that they have an individual style which marks them out, or that there is a happy marriage between the content of the piece they are singing and their style of delivery. For a number of years we have been running public workshops for actors, singers and their teachers on vocal style in musical theatre. The four key elements that we have identified will enable you to deliver your song in the right style for the show you are auditioning for. This includes taking songs from one style category across to another by adjusting your vocal style and musical style.

There are many different genres of musical around at the moment written in different musical styles. Lets begin with the overview: types of musical. Since it is staged, a musical is first and foremost a dramatic event, so we have defined the different categories of musical by their dramatic style.

SEVEN CATEGORIES OF MUSICAL

The verismo musical

This is a gritty heightened drama with a strong storyline. The key feature is in the style of language and the delivery, which is dramatic, strong and contemporary. Think soap opera writ large on stage and you have the dramatic feel. *Les Misérables* is the archetypal verismo musical with its strong storyline, gritty drama, and a focus on close character work, pulling the audience in. Many of the verismo shows are through-composed: there is very little or no spoken text, and the libretto is set to music throughout. A variety of subject matter can be dealt with verismo style: *Les Misérables* is a classic nineteenth century novel whereas *Miss Saigon* is based on *Madame Butterfly* (an early twentieth century verismo opera). Both musicals are in verismo style. Sondheim's treatment of the tale of *Sweeney Todd* broke new ground when it opened on Broadway and still has the capacity to shock modern audiences.

The sketch musical

There is often no through-line to the plot, just a series of sketches. The singers usually play different characters throughout the performance, although there may be one linking character acting as a narrator. *Smokey Joe's Café* is a great example of a sketch show; so is *Personals*, with the song lyrics written by the writers of *Friends*. The emphasis is on the songs as vignettes. Usually there is a loose link between songs by virtue of the show's title (e.g. *Elegies for Angels, Punks and Raging Queens*) or a central theme. Other sketch shows include *A is for Alice, Closer Than Ever, Dreamgirls*, and *Blues in the Night*.

The tribute musical

The usual focus of a tribute show is to showcase one person, group or their music. (You might say that *Smokey Joe's Café*, which celebrates the music of Lieber and Stoller, is a tribute show in sketch style.) There is often a storyline, although sometimes it does not extend into the second half. Generally a company of characters interact with each other to make up the action. *Buddy* is one of the great tribute musicals: many of the characters remain the same throughout the first half, which differentiates it from a sketch show. The second half of the show becomes a concert. Tribute shows can also have less of an emphasis on storyline, and more on the interaction of the various characters. Other tribute shows include *Mamma Mia, Patsy Cline, Five Guys Named Mo, The Best of Times*, and the dance show *Fosse*.

The classic book musical

Unlike the early musical comedies in which the plot is fashioned around the songs, the great book musicals enable both the action and the characters to develop *through* song. Rodgers and Hammerstein wrote classic book musicals starting with *Oklahoma!* and finishing with *The Sound of Music*. Other examples are *Guys and Dolls*, *My Fair Lady*, *West Side Story*, *She Loves Me*, *Annie* and the first musical written specifically for television, *Cinderella*.

The movie musical

This is a musical that started off as a movie with songs and incidental music. The format may be based on the book musical or on the concept musical. Examples include *Victor Victoria*, *Calamity Jane*, *Singing in the Rain*, *Seven Brides for Seven Brothers*, *Dr Dolittle*, and the Disney cartoons *Beauty and the Beast* and *The Lion King*.

The concept musical

This is a show that starts with an idea, rather than a pre-existing plot. The idea may come from an historical event (e.g. *Assassins*, *Evita*, and *Jesus Christ Superstar*), reflect an aspect of contemporary life (e.g. *Company*, *Hair*, *Romance Romance*, and *A Chorus Line*), or be based loosely around a film, play or book (e.g. *Nine*, *Martin Guerre*, *Follies*, *The Secret Garden*, *Phantom of the Opera*, and *The Witches of Eastwick*). The concept show is the most prevalent form for musicals today. Many songs from concept shows can be used for auditions for other types of musical because the range is so wide. The difference between the concept show and the sketch show is that there is usually a plot (though arguably not in *Hair*) and roles for named characters who interact with one another.

Cabaret

This is a style of its own, needing the performer to acknowledge and work with the audience by going beyond the 'fourth wall' (an imaginary wall between the audience and the front of the playing or stage area). The fourth wall preserves the reality of the dramatic situation that the performers are in, so that the characters do not know that the audience is there. A cabaret artist, even when playing a character, will work beyond the fourth wall to contact the audience directly (think of *An Evening With Shirley Bassey* or *An*

Evening With Michael Ball).

Many plays and musicals contain songs or characters that break the convention of the fourth wall, albeit momentarily, for dramatic purposes, e.g. the Engineer in *Miss Saigon*, Balladeer in *Assassins* and the Street Singer in *Threepenny Opera*. In each instance these characters serve an important dramatic function, enabling the audience to disengage from the action of the story.

For our purposes any song that is performed or written to cross the fourth wall between singer and audience can be identified as cabaret, even if musically it comes from one of the other categories. If the singer is contacting the audience and responding directly to them, the song is in cabaret style. Cabaret style songs can be very useful for certain sorts of audition, e.g. TIE, pantomime, or any situation where a song is used as a teaching vehicle.

Match the job to your skills

What are the implications of dramatic style for you as a performer and auditionee? Know the genre of musical you are planning to audition for. The verismo musical suits a performer with strong dramatic skills; dance is not emphasised. The same will be true of many concept musicals, particularly those by Sondheim. However, there are exceptions such as *A Chorus Line* and *Chicago* that are clearly dance-based and will require dancer-singers. Some of the older book musicals require a mixed company of dancer-singers, singer-dancers and singer-actors. In the movie musicals, characterisation is important. When you plan to audition for a movie musical, decide whether is it based on the concept format or the book musical. The tribute and sketch shows place a greater emphasis on good singing skills in the right vocal style, stage presence and the right look. An exception to this would be *Fosse*, which is a tribute show to the choreography of Bob Fosse and obviously requires strong dance skills above everything. Tribute shows might well be looking for cabaret singers, actor-singers and sometimes, performers from the pop and tribute band circuit. Some tribute shows will specify that they don't want mainstream musical theatre singers because they are seeking a different vocal style or a different look. It's important that you check out the requirements of the show you are auditioning for and match it with your own skills. Either your agent, PCR[1] or the representative of the casting director should be able to give you a detailed breakdown on what is required.

[1] Production and Casting Report published weekly by PCR Ltd

TYPES OF SONG

When you go to an audition the most common request is for you to bring two songs: a ballad and an uptempo number. Sometimes the brief is for two contrasting songs. Part of the dramatic and musical interest in musicals is in the different types of song, and it is important that you have all the main types of song covered in your audition portfolio. We have kept our song categories under the broad umbrellas of ballad and uptempo, simply because these are the ones most often asked for by your agent and the auditions listed in the trade papers. There are many other ways of categorising songs; one of the most interesting that is also practical is described by David Craig in his book *A Performer Prepares* in which he lists twelve categories of song and a thirteenth for contemporary pop.

Ballad

A ballad is generally lyrical, of a slow to medium tempo, sustained, and a vehicle for vocal and emotional communication. It is often about love, but not always (e.g. *'God on High'* from *Les Misérables* and *'There are worse things I could do'* from *Grease*). A ballad may have a contrasting section that is in a faster tempo or verse style, but it still inhabits the ballad territory. There are at least five ballad types:

1. The torch song

This is a highly charged emotional ballad, heightened in delivery, and usually a uni-focus song. (For the definition of uni-focus see Chapter 9.) A torch song is often linked with a particular singer.

Examples include *'The Man that Got Away'* (*A Star Is Born* as recorded by Judy Garland), *'I Who Have Nothing'* (Mogol & Donida, Lieber & Stoller, as recorded by Shirley Bassey), *'If you go away'* (Jacques Brel), and *'Delilah'* (Mason and Smith, as recorded by Tom Jones).

2. The dramatic ballad

This has a dramatic storyline and is often a soliloquy. It may also be a turning point in the action or development of a character.

Examples include *'Meadowlark'* (*The Baker's Wife*), *'And the World Goes Round'* (*New York, New York*), *'Who Is This Man?'* – Javert's suicide (*Les Misérables*), *'Being Alive'* (*Company*), and *'My Friends'* (*Sweeney Todd*).

3. The waltz ballad

These are written in triple time, and were made popular by Rodgers and Hammerstein. Sondheim has written modern versions in several of his musicals.

Examples include '*Out of My Dreams*' (*Oklahoma!*), '*Ten Minutes Ago*' (*Cinderella*), '*One More Kiss*' (*Follies*), and '*Remember*' (*A Little Night Music*).

4. The swing ballad

The vocal line will still be slow and sustained with the accompaniment providing an easy swing element.

'*The Girls of Summer*' (*Marry Me a Little*), '*Someone to Watch Over Me*' (*Oh, Kay!*), and '*Dance a Little Closer*' (*Dance a Little Closer*).

5. The rock or pop ballad

These examples are all from musical theatre, but there is nothing to stop you taking a pop song to your audition if rock or pop has been requested.

'*Whistle Down the Wind*' (*Whistle Down the Wind*), '*I Don't Know How to Love Him*' (*Jesus Christ Superstar*), and '*Can You Feel the Love Tonight?*' (*The Lion King*).

When looking at sheet music don't be fooled by the fast passage work of some of the contemporary artistes such as Whitney Houston and Celine Dion. Songs like '*The Reason*' and '*I Will Always Love You*' are still ballads even though there are a lot of fast notes there. These notes are meant to be sung as embellishments to the main melody and do not upset the slow feel of the music.

Uptempo

This includes anything that's not a ballad! It can range from moderate to fast tempo. A key feature is that the rhythm shares importance with the melody or may even pre-empt it. Note that the figuration of the accompaniment is often the true indicator, even if the vocal part is not actually all that fast-moving.

There are five different types of uptempo numbers that we can identify:

1. The patter song

There is a fast feel (even at moderate speed) because of the very wordy, rapid speech patterns. The patter song is often driven and frenetic. It is a verbal tour-de-force, usually on one subject. Words take precedence over rhythm.

Examples include '*I'm Not Getting Married Today*' (*Company*), '*Another Hundred People*' (*Company*), '*Now*' (*A Little Night Music*), and '*If*' (*Two On the Aisle*).

2. The point number

This has a narrative and is wordy, but is not as fast as the patter song. A point number focuses on storyline, detail and repartee. There is often a place for the audience to 'get' the point.

Examples include '*I Think I May Want to Remember Today*' (*Starting Here Starting Now*), '*Master of the House*' (*Les Misérables*), '*Nothing*' (*A Chorus Line*), and '*Crossword Puzzle*' (*Starting Here Starting Now*).

3. The true up tempo number

This is characterised by fast speed in the repetitive, rhythmic (oompah) accompaniment. Without it, the vocal line can sound more like a ballad. Don't be fooled! Company numbers can also work as a solo if the parts are mostly in unison and the text allows.

Examples include '*The Trolley Song*' (*Meet Me In St Louis*), '*Wherever he ain't*' (*Mack and Mabel*), '*Luck Be a Lady*' (*Guys and Dolls*), '*I Cain't Say No*' (*Oklahoma!*), '*Johnny One Note*' (*Babes In Arms*), '*Greased Lightning*' (*Grease*), '*Two People In Love*' (*Baby*), '*Oklahoma!*' (*Oklahoma!*), and '*No Business Like Show Business*' (*Annie Get Your Gun*).

4. Swing and ragtime

These have a moderate to fast dance rhythm, with the accompaniment providing the swing element. Many Gershwin and Berlin numbers fall into this category.

Examples include '*Someone to Watch Over Me*' (*Oh, Kay!*), '*Learn Your Lessons Well*' (*Godspell*), '*American Dream*' (*Miss Saigon*), '*Miss Byrd*' (*Closer Than Ever*), and '*Herod's Song*' (*Jesus Christ Superstar*).

5. The dramatic uptempo

This often has a contrasting slow section but still inhabits the territory of uptempo. Company numbers also fall into this category.

'*Proud Lady*' (*The Baker's Wife*), '*Be On Your Own*' (*Nine*), '*How Did I End Up Here?*' (*Romance Romance*), '*If You Want To Die In Bed*' (*Miss Saigon*), '*At The End Of The Day*' (*Les Misérables*), and the seconnd act finale of *Threepenny Opera*.

Now you can cross-check the categories of musical with the types of song. You will find that you do not need to keep rigidly within the categories; the important thing is to understand the dramatic style of the show you are auditioning for. This will enable you to target the material that is not only suitable for you, but also for the audition. But what if you are singing the right song for the right musical in the wrong style? Read on.

Chapter 7

What Is Style?

You do not need to read music to understand about musical style; you need only to use your ears. Let's start by looking at some of the factors that arise when we think about style.

1. How can you identify it?
2. What is needed to change it?
3. How accurate is your style?
4. What could you do if asked to perform your song in a different style?
5. Can the same songs be used for different auditions?

Why style is important

LA was auditioning for the singer-dancer roles in Gershwin musicals, and sang '*If I Loved You*' in the style of '*Stand By Me*'. He did so very well, but he wasn't getting the jobs. He needed to sing in the style of the job he was auditioning for. '*If I Loved You*' is classic book musical style and '*Stand By Me*' is pop.

MC puts on his own productions and had done leads in the West End. He gets recalled for Cameron Macintosh productions but has been told that he sings in the wrong style: too much vibrato, too lyric, too smooth. He was very comfortable with the Broadway concept and classic book musicals and needed to present a more verismo style of performing.

GM was a very experienced performer who had the musical style of verismo but not the vocal set-up. She was pasting a contemporary musical theatre style on top of her classical 'legit' sound and ran into difficulties. By sorting this out, she was able to move from covering a small role in a verismo musical to second lead.

MG had a featured role in a tribute musical and was a great rock 'n' roll singer with loads of onstage charisma. He also had a good rock tenor voice but knew he could not sing Enjolras in *Les Misérables*, even though he felt he was the right casting for it (which he was). We identified a need to work on the appropriate style for a more verismo drama.

All of these are examples of working professionals who needed to reassess their level of competence in order to increase their versatility. By helping them to identify the musical and vocal hallmarks of style, they were able to move on in their careers.

DEFINING MUSICAL STYLE

Music is a language. Each musical style has its own flavour or what we call 'feel', just as a Shakespearean sonnet or a Restoration comedy does. To demonstrate this, we are going to use the first few bars of 'This Is the Moment' from *Jekyll and Hyde*.

This   is   the   mo - ment   This   is   the   day

Let's begin the process by identifying the style of 'This Is the Moment', using the three elements already examined.
1. Dramatic style: sufficiently gritty and dramatic to fall into the verismo category. This is definitely not cabaret or classic book.
2. Song type: ballad, with simple structure and a long, slow build.
3. Musical style: the publishing date is 1990 and the musical is by Frank Wildhorn. This is significant because Wildhorn has written for numerous pop artists including Whitney Houston (e.g. 'Where Do Broken Hearts Go?'). So, while the song comes from a verismo musical, it could also be classed as a dramatic pop ballad, which indicates a contemporary sound. For musical style, you can move from verismo through contemporary concept to pop without compromising the style of writing. The song can stand alone, since the lyrics of the song are not specific to the plot.
Now look at some of the musical factors that contribute to style.

Rhythm and pitch

These two factors are what differentiate sung from spoken text. Just as an actor has to find his way around iambic pentameter, other verse forms and archaic language, the actor who sings must find his or her way around the musical style of any given song.

This song has four crotchets or quarter notes (beats) to each bar: the first beat in each bar feels the strongest, followed by beat three, then two and four.
1. Syllables set on long notes tend to stand out more than short ones.

The longest note in this extract is '-ment'.

2. Syllables set on a strong beat will also become emphasised: 'This' and 'mo-' are set on the beat, with 'mo-' being the stronger as it is on the first beat of the bar.

3. Syllables set on higher pitches will be more prominent since high notes are heard as louder. The lowest note is on 'This', and the highest on '-ment'.

So both the rhythmic setting and the pitch affect the stressing of the words. In this example rhythm, stress, and pitch give conflicting signals. Part of your job as a performer is to interpret these signals.

The interpretations you can make fall into three broad categories: shape of words, shape of phrases, and shape of the landscape.

1. In singing, interpreting the shape of words includes grading volume and intensity of vowels between syllables, different ways of using diphthongs, elongating or shortening consonants. Your decisions can be led by the flavour or emotional content of individual words as well as their semantic meaning.

2. Interpreting the shape of phrases includes dynamic grading between words and phrases, length of held notes and decay, backphrasing, and rubato. This can be led by the specific intention of phrases and sentences. (*Why* am I saying it?)

3. Interpreting the shape of the landscape includes overall tempo, over-all feel, type of orchestration, grading of intensity throughout the story, and altering sections of music. This can be led by the 'big picture', the general storyline and overall emotional complexity of the situation. Remember that each song is a tiny one-act play and that you or the audience must be in a different place by the end of it.

Word shaping

Here's how to avoid upsetting the natural stress of the words in our sample line:

1. Voice the 'TH' of 'this' on the same pitch as the vowel. This will help you pitch the note correctly and will stop scooping from beneath.

2. Put a glottal before '-is': it makes the word stand out to have that tiny stop before it. You also avoid 'thissis' (rhymes with mrs).

3. Voice the 'TH' of 'the' on the same pitch as the following vowel (see above).

4. Voice the first 'M' of 'mo-' on the pitch of the following vowel. Elongate the consonant by starting it early (finish the word 'the' sooner). It is the vowel that is on the beat, so the consonant must come before the beat, which means stealing some of the time from

the previous word. If you constantly put the consonant on the beat, the musical director will think either that you always want everything slower, or that you simply cannot sing in time.

Reshaping to change your style

Experiment with the diphthong in 'moment'. A diphthong is characterised by the transition between two component sounds. Say this syllable slowly to get the feel of the transition. In the examples that follow you will be experimenting with the timing of the transition and how this affects sung text. We are representing the two component sounds as 'aw' and 'ou'.

Here are four different versions.

1. Make the transition between the first and second vowel slowly ('maw---ou') and then finish the word.
2. Now make the transition quickly and reach the second vowel early ('mawou--') and finish the word.
3. Now hold the first vowel longer, then move quickly to the second sound ('m-aw-ou').
4. Now don't put a diphthong in at all ('maw'). You would never speak the syllable like this, but it is not uncommon to hear it sung.

You can do any of these versions in real time. Notice the difference in style or feel that result. Version 2 sometimes appears in pop singing; version 4 tends to appear in classical singing, where the diphthong is often ignored (not something we recommend even to our classical singers). We prefer either version 3 or, for clarity and audience comprehension, version 1.

Here are some further options for working the consonants that have stylistic implications.

1. In the word 'moment' pitch the second 'm' on the note you have just left (the E). You will find that you slide up to the upper note after you have started the last syllable. Some pop recording artists have adopted this style so watch out for it in pop and tribute musicals. This is sometimes called 'scooping'.

   Now pitch the 'm' of '-ment' on the note you are going to (the F#). This is more appropriate to classic book musicals (a cleaner musical outline) and verismo (more immediacy of text). It also makes the upper notes easier to sing.
2. Likewise, sing the 'nt' of '-ment' on a lower pitch than the 'me'. In rehearsing this you might like to think ahead to the note you will sing on your next 'this' (a whole five notes lower than the written pitch of '-ment'). Although this is not always done deliberately, it gives an impression of sagging, of tiredness, disillusion, or attitude.

Now sing the 'nt' on the same pitch as the 'me'. The first version is useful in some rock and pop ballads, but completely inappropriate to classic book style. This is sometimes called 'falling off the note'. The second version is again more appropriate to styles that need immediacy of text and cleaner lines, and also makes the notes easier to sing.

3. Sing 'mehnt'. Now sing 'muhnt'. By singing the second, neutral vowel, you can disguise the fact that the unimportant syllable of the word 'moment' is placed on a higher and longer note.

4. Sing the '-ment' louder than the 'mo-' (as implied in the musical text). Now sing the '-ment' softer than the 'mo-'. Notice the difference between these two versions: if you follow the contours of the music, the text of the song becomes less specific and more a vehicle for the voice and a generalised feeling. Version 2 follows the contours of the text.

Although you need more control to execute the changes in stages 1 and 2 and the graded dynamic version of stage 4, you will be following more closely the pattern of speech without sacrificing the given rhythm. You will maintain the integrity of both musical and verbal text, which is essential for any musical where the songs are there to serve the story and not the other way around. This means any verismo or book musical and the majority of the concept musicals.

The point of dissecting the execution of this one word 'moment' has been to alert you to vocal style habits. A vocal style habit would be a personal nuance that you use habitually, either because you like it, or because it makes singing easier for you, or because this is the way you have been trained. Mostly we are not aware of our vocal style habits. Notice which of the above examples came most naturally to you. You would be surprised how often an actor may not get through the second or third recall because they demonstrate vocal style habits that are inappropriate to the musical they are auditioning for. Unless the musical team is convinced that you are able to change style, they will look for someone else. In pop singing vocal style habits are desirable: they stamp the singer with individuality. In almost all types of musical theatre (even pop tribute show) you will need to be able to sing in the style of the music and demonstrate your individuality through dramatic interpretation and voice colour.

Phrasing

Because sung text involves music phrasing as well as word, you need to make sure that your dynamic levels convey what you intend.

Changing your dynamic levels within a phrase can give a different reading. There are two features that can make a phrase 'peak': the composer sets a word or set of words on a strong beat and higher note, or you sing the word and the note louder than the rest of the phrase (or grade your dynamic towards this note).

1. Example a (opposite): the most important word is 'day' (this is it, it's almost a surprise). This is fairly easy to do, as 'day' is on the highest note in the phrase, and will therefore be heard as louder.
   Example b: the most important word is 'this' (today is the culmination of many days). This needs a little more control, as you need to sing 'day' softer than the rest of the sentence in order to feature the words on lower notes. Note that in both examples you need to sing '-ment' much softer than anything else in order to take the focus away from it.

2. There are two ways of dealing with long notes: rhythm (hold them for their full value, elongate, or cut them short) and intensity (decay, sustain or increase). Holding the note for its full value without changing the intensity gives a more classical impression of line. However, ironically, some recording artists have adopted this style, and it is making a comeback in the pop musical. This may be because the function of song in pop is somewhat different from that of song in musical theatre.

3. Decay is very useful in singing as it can give the sense of spoken phrasing to sung pitches without resorting to Rex Harrison-type clipped delivery. In both examples a and b we have included an instruction for decay. Even if you start the '-ment' softly you will need to do something with it because it is one of the longest notes in the phrase. If you increase the volume and intensity, you will draw attention to a weak syllable. Once you have arrived on the note (softly), decrease the volume and intensity without losing the pitch or the vowel. Decay is not the same as falling off the note since the pitch remains the same.

Backphrasing and rubato

Example c shows an example of backphrasing. In backphrasing certain words and notes are elongated, stretching the phrase beyond its original proportions.

In this example, although you start on the same beat as before, everything else arrives late, and the rhythm and shape of the original phrase is changed out of all recognition. Some actors do backphrasing in the belief that they are staying closer to the text. Unfortunately this is done at the expense of the music and might drive your musical

This Is The Moment

Key: **p** = soft/gentle
          mp = moderately soft
          mf = moderately loud
          f = loud/strong
          ⟩ = getting softer

a

b

c

d

director mad in performance. Others insert backphrasing because they like the feel of the tune and want to expand it. Unfortunately this is done at the expense of the text, and it is not suitable for songs and musicals that are text driven. However, if the focus of the song is as a vehicle for the singer and their voice, then backphrasing would be appropriate. An example would be '*What I Did For Love*' (*A Chorus Line*), which was specifically written to be released as a single.

Example d shows rubato, used to emphasise in different ways. Rubato differs from backphrasing in two ways: rubato alters the rhythm *within* the phrase but does not alter the overall length, and singer and accompaniment can rubato together. Singer and accompaniment both doing backphrasing is a disaster! 'This' is shortened and 'is' is moved forwards to elongate it without losing momentum, then 'this' is elongated for further emphasis, and 'is the' is sung very short and fast. Note that 'moment' and 'day' remain in the same place as in the original. Time has been taken from the surrounding words without changing the overall length of the phrase. Some composers, including Sondheim, write in the rubato they want; some leave it to the performer. We find it best to notice what is written first before changing it. A great example of this is Sondheim's '*Not a Day Goes By*' (*Merrily We Roll Along*), which includes eighteen indications of time change and numerous instructions to change dynamic.

To summarise our points about backphrasing: if the main vehicle is voice and the song, then backphrasing may be stylistically appropriate. If not, then words, sense and meaning come first, and we recommend that you use decay and rubato instead.

Landscaping

Landscaping describes the peaks and troughs of a song, taking in emotional and dynamic highs and releases in both the text and the music, changes of tempo and feel, changes of tessitura, and changes of orchestration or piano part.

For landscaping we must consider the whole song. Here are some general points:

The tempo marking is slow, and the piece is in four. The accompaniment begins quietly and ends loudly. The vocal range is from low B to high G#. The tessitura (range of notes that most of the voice part sits in) is low to begin with and climbs to sit high in the range for the last two pages. The implication of this is that the general level of intensity increases throughout the song. It is interesting to note that the highest note in the song (G#) occurs only two thirds of the way through, and is relatively short; it is not the highest point in the story or the musical text. We are going to deal with tempo and 'feel' separately, even though one can affect the other. Throughout the piece, the phrasing is constructed in a similar way, with a few shorter notes followed by a long stressed note, usually at the end of the phrase. So structurally the song is very simple, perhaps indicating that the singer is obsessed by one idea.

1. **Tempo and feel.** The sustained notes are the key to the slow extremes of speed: too slow, and the performer will spend all his energy worrying about the next breath. Likewise, the short notes are the key to the fast extremes of speed: too fast and the words and notes will be gabbled and lost. You will find that, rather than there being a 'perfect' tempo that must be reproduced every time you sing, you can still give a good performance with tempo variations either way. More important than tempo is 'feel'.

   It is possible to play in exactly the 'right' tempo but with the wrong feel, and that can be very confusing for inexperienced performers. You might find it helpful to think of feel being more like pace in a dramatic context, rather than the speed of the delivery. An experienced audition pianist will be quite used to such motivational phrases as 'it drives forwards', 'held back', 'funky', 'quiet and intense', 'a rock feel', 'swing' (even when it isn't a swing number). This particular piece has a feel of suppressed energy, so there is a rhythmic tension about it that says 'slow but not relaxed', 'moving forwards but not speeding up'.

2. **Orchestration and piano reductions.** Although in an audition you will not have to deal with an orchestra, it is worth noticing what type of feel the accompaniment has. In a rehearsal period for a show, the first time cast gets together with the band is always incredibly exciting; it is the first time you can experience the musical subtext in full. Show orchestrations can be lush strings, punchy brass, or spiky percussion, and this can add to your performance.

   Piano parts from the complete show score are usually rendered-down versions of the score, and will contain as much detail as one person with two hands can play! Songbooks on the other hand tend to have easier piano reductions, as historically songbooks were designed for the home market and amateur pianists. Often the key of a song will be changed to make the piano part easier – odd but true. This is where a cast album is useful, not to learn the mannerisms of that one performer, but to get the flavour (and key) of the whole piece. Listen out for the type of instrument accompanying your chosen song. Hopefully your pianist(s) will know what type of instrumentation is used, but it is better to research this yourself and not rely on someone else. It is no good going vocally and dramatically full out on something that actually only has viola and banjo in the band. Conversely, in '*Daddy's Hands*' (*Ragtime*), the lines 'the blood and the pain, the anger and pain, I buried my heart in the ground' are over a full orchestra playing fortissimo (very strong), so a breathy falsetto quality simply will not work. You have to scale your performance to the level of support from the orchestra as well as to that point in the storyline.

Putting the landscape together

Now let's examine '*This Is the Moment*' as a whole.
1. The orchestration starts quietly, with a slow moving bass line and a rhythmic moving accompaniment.
2. There is a key change where the orchestration changes to block chords played forte (strong) with a dotted rhythm in the bass line, reflecting in the music the slightly unsteady, slightly manic character.

The level of instrumentation and volume at each point in the song can give you guidelines to the peaks and troughs in the landscape of the song. The shaping of the story is important on several levels: the landscape of the whole song will have ebbs and flows, and will usually reach some sort of conclusion. Within that ebb and flow, each phrase will have its own ebb and flow to make sense of the more specific emotions that the character feels moment by moment. And within those moments are the shaping of individual words and syllables with their specific meaning and flavour. In '*This Is the Moment*', the title phrase occurs seven times. Each one needs to be different to read well, either in intensity, volume, shape, meaning, or emphasis. Exploring on all these levels, both textual and musical, will put the audience in touch with the emotional story of the character *within* the song.

Using the accompaniment to change style

If you wish to move the song into a different category, the easiest way is to change the accompaniment, in rhythm and feel. You can either sing in the same style as before, or alter your style in sync with the pianist. We are not talking here about getting a new arrangement for your song (though that is certainly an option), merely about indicating on the music a few simple changes that will alter the feel. A good audition pianist will not find this difficult provided you have marked up your music clearly. Here is an example: '*Habañera*' from *Carmen Jones*.

Habañera 1

Habañera 2

In the second version Jeremy simply changed the habañera rhythm to a bossa nova rhythm: the speed and beat stay the same, but the feel is much busier, more lively and more urgent. The singer can now either sing the habañera feel or join in with the more urgent bossa nova.

You can also keep the rhythm the same but change the speed. If you take an uptempo swing and slow it down, you get a swing ballad – effectively two songs in one. Many of the Gershwin standards were written as uptempo swing, but were recreated as swing ballad or torch songs by Ella Fitzgerald. In the Sondheim show *Follies*, 'Broadway Baby' is sung as uptempo swing, part of a trio of songs sung simultaneously. When performed as a solo number it is invariably sung much slower as a swing ballad. Note that we listed '*Someone To Watch Over Me*' under swing ballad *and* swing uptempo; you can change the feel by changing the speed. Another option is to do the beginning of a song 'colla voce' (that is sung in a free rhythm according to the feel of the words) with a few simple chords as accompaniment. This enables you to make an impact with a change of pace when the song moves into 'tempo' (rhythmic time). '*I Think I May Want To Remember Today*' from *Starting Here Starting Now* usually starts at full speed, but it is possible to do a more thoughtful version, building in excitement, by singing the first thirty-two bars colla voce, speeding up into the rest of the song.

I Think I May Want To Remember Today

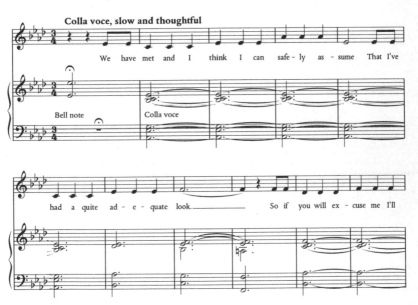

go to my room And write all this down in my book.____ For

oh,____ I

A tempo

pp   cresc.

think I may want to re - mem - ber____ to - day____ etc.

mf   f   etc.   etc.

VOCAL STYLE

You will see mentioned in several chapters the importance of being able to change voice quality in different situations. Changes in voice quality can denote a number of things: a specific musical style, a character choice, or a dramatic change within a song (word and phrase painting). In this chapter we will be looking at how you can change voice quality to change style of musical and musical style. If you look again at the real-life examples we gave you about the importance of style on page 58, you will realise that some of the work we did with these actors was on changing their voice quality. What does this mean?

Whenever you are singing or speaking you are making some kind of voice quality. Your voice quality can be measured scientifically and identified. So, at a very simple level, someone with a rather shrill piercing voice might be identified as using twang quality; someone with a low, melodious voice might be using sob. Actors use different voice qualities all the time on stage as part of their means of expressing characterisation and nuance of text. There is a brief overview of the voice qualities on pp 23-4, but if you want to read about these qualities in detail, we suggest you refer to *Singing and The Actor*, Chapter 12.

Changing your style for different auditions

If you choose to do '*This Is the Moment*' as an exercise, sing it in a key that is mostly in your comfort zone. Girls will want to do it down a third or fourth, baritones should be able to manage it in the given key but can transpose down a tone if needed.

Suggested voice qualities

The verismo dramatic style is direct, drawing the audience in. Look for moments of contrast in the song and use changes of voice quality for dramatic effect. It's extremely important that you maintain the integrity of the text by making sure you do not distort words or run them together. Do not be afraid to use marked changes of dynamic from phrase to phrase if it makes sense with the text.

Here are some contraindications of verismo vocal style
1. Do not join all the notes together in one phrase making a long line. This is a hallmark of classical singing style and compromises the text.
2. Do not sing with a low larynx: it will make you sound operatic, and this is too far away from verismo.
3. Avoid backphrasing and sliding between the notes. Also avoid falling off the notes, or scooping from underneath. These belong to contemporary pop style.

A suggested vocal journey through the song might employ cry quality (produced very quietly) or falsetto for the moments of intense anticipation or self-revelation. Speech quality is useful for the moments that are less heightened, whereas twang might be used to intensify the mood. Speech and twang mixed always produce a strong, dramatic effect and belt is suitable for the climax of the song. Do not be afraid to use large dynamic contrasts in this style.

Changing your vocal style

Let's suppose that you are using the song to audition for a concept musical that is written in a contemporary pop style. (It might be for example Andrew Lloyd Webber's *Whistle Down The Wind*). This song works well as a dramatic pop ballad. Here are some indications of what we would expect to hear in a pop ballad, as well as contraindications.

1. Avoid cry quality unless it is mixed with speech, giving that soulful ballad feel.
2. Avoid singing with a low larynx; it is too operatic. (The pop exceptions to this are Cher and Heather Small, the lead singer of M People, who both sing with low larynx but without cry.)
3. Twang, nasal twang and twang mixed with speech are all acceptable for the louder more passionate sections. If the song is high enough for you, you could use belt at the end.
4. Look at opportunities for backphrasing and sliding on and off pitches to give that more laid back feel.

You will see that the voice qualities are not dissimilar to our original reading of the song; what has changed is the vocal landscaping. The peaks and troughs in verismo vocal style are more marked and dramatic, whereas the pop ballad will be characterised by a long slow build.

Now, suppose you had been asked to sing this song in audition for a classic book musical; what would you have to change? Key factors for a ballad in this style are sweetness of tone, bloom on the long notes, warmth and intensity. Sweetness of tone and warmth indicate cry quality. It won't be mixed with speech, but twang can be added for volume and intensity (not nasal twang). Towards the end of the song you might become more operatic to match the grandiose language of the character. 'Bloom' on the long notes means letting the sound grow and maybe decay again on the long notes; they should not sound 'straight'. There is an overall feel of evenness of tone, and the dynamic changes during phrases happen within this.

Doing your research

Whatever stage you are at in your career, when you learn new material you will need to do your research. Nobody can know everything, and if you are presented with the task of learning a new genre then it is up to you to find out as much as you can about it. Only then can you feel confident when you go to audition. Go to musicals, buy recordings of musicals, listen to music on the radio, and criticise and analyse what you hear. Learn songs just as you read text; even if you eventually discard them you will have gained something by the process.

Chapter 8

Your Portfolio

In this chapter we show you how to build an audition portfolio. Your audition portfolio is taken from your personal database of songs. It needs to be chosen with care and updated to match your personal skills, personal development, career shifts and any trends in your area of work. In building your portfolio you will need to cross-reference the information you have gathered from previous chapters about your job description and level of competence, voice type, casting category and what makes you special. In addition to this you will need to categorise your songs by musical (verismo, classic book and so on) and by song type (ballad, uptempo and their subdivisions).

Deciding on your portfolio

We have found that many actors have a reasonable database of songs, but are unclear about the criteria for deciding which ones should go in their portfolio. You cannot expect to keep twenty songs on the boil to audition standard. The idea of having a database is that you can add to it all the time. Your portfolio, however, should remain the same for eighteen months to two years, so that all the songs in it are always ready for audition. You should be prepared to update the portfolio after this period, though it is likely you will do some songs for many years. If a particular song gets you through to the next round, why change it?

Most casting directors and directors like to hear you first doing a song of your own choice, in the genre of the musical you are auditioning for. Your own choice of song tells them what type of voice you have, the level of your vocal skill and your performing comfort zone. We cannot emphasise enough that the songs in your audition portfolio (which we assume to be songs that you take for a first hearing) must be in your *FOAL* area and vocal comfort zone. You need to know which songs in your portfolio are suitable for which style category, and this means doing your research.

Checklist for making your portfolio

Using the information in Chapter 5, find twenty songs that have the potential to be in your *FOAL* area.

1. Discard any songs that strongly contradict your current casting (e.g. if you are obviously too young or the wrong physical type). Remember that you can rework a song by giving it a new reading for certain types of audition (check the job descriptions in Chapter 2).
2. Discard any songs that are not within your vocal range and capabilities (see Chapters 3 and 4). Put songs that you like but don't feel ready to sing on the back burner. Remember that under certain circumstances it is fine to transpose standards and pop songs.
3. Discard or put to one side any songs that have difficult accompaniments. Check this out with your song coach or singing teacher. If you are really attached to a song with a tricky accompaniment and feel that it shows you off well, keep it for those occasions when you can afford to take a pianist with you.
4. Earmark one song as 'easy accompaniment' and always have it with you as a back-up.
5. Using the information in Chapter 6, divide your songs into ballad and uptempo. Make a note of any songs that you also think can be reworked by changing the feel of the accompaniment. Check that you have a good balance of ballads and uptempo songs.
6. Make a note of the musicals category for which you can use each song (see Chapter 6). Remember that many songs can cross categories.
7. Make sure that you have material that is going to be useful for the kind of work you expect to be doing (look at the work categories in Chapter 2).
8. Decide which songs may need cutting because they are too long. Note that cuts for open calls can be made when you are getting ready to memorise.

Here is a detailed profile of a performer, taking you through the process of making your portfolio step-by-step. We have included information about category of musical and song type.

Profile of an actor-singer RD (female, 28 years old)

1. Level of competence
   Fringe lead, touring named part, West End understudy, character roles in quality pantomime and variety spots as a featured artist. She also did TV and film, and would be suitable for roles that might require some singing in this field (see Chapter 2).

2. Vocal skills

    Good range and command of several voice qualities. Actual range: Eb below middle C to high Bb; working range: Low F to high G. Her vocal comfort zone was in the speech quality range Bb below Middle C to the C a ninth above, and she had a good strong belt quality to D a tone above that (see Chapter 3).

3. Voice type

    Mezzo-soprano. Her sound was thick and strong, and she had worked to develop brightness. Her voice fitted her casting type of young character, and her playing range was twenty-five to forty years and older. As a character actress she did not need to demonstrate strong lyric singing, but she enjoyed doing patter and narrative songs with a comic or dramatic twist, as well as jazz standards. One of her strengths was in being able to give a new slant on a standard song (see Chapter 4).

4. The interview questions revealed the following key phrases:

    Ordinary woman in extraordinary or unusual circumstances. Pragmatic, sense of irony, quick changes of thought process, strength and humour.

5. From this profile we amassed a database of twenty songs that would be in her *FOAL* area in terms of dramatic content (see Chapter 5).

    i. '*Funny Valentine*' from *Babes in Arms*.
        • Classic book, now a standard.
        • Intelligent woman ballad that can be played with a variety of subtexts.
        • Useful for many types of audition, either as a first or second song, but check your key!

    ii. '*But Not For Me*' from *Girl Crazy* and *Crazy For You*.
        • Classic book or musical comedy.
        • Ballad or swing ballad with wry humour, *not* heart on sleeve! The tempo can be changed from swing to swing-ballad or slower still for torch song.

    iii. '*Naughty Baby*' from *Crazy For You*.
        • Classic book or musical comedy.
        • An uptempo swing number.
        • Comedy vamp character.

    iv. '*Moments in the Woods*' from *Into The Woods*.
        • Concept musical.
        • An uptempo point number.
        • No special musical style points.
        • Quick changes of thought. Pragmatic rather than earthy with comic irony.

v.   '*Saga of Jenny*' from *Lady in the Dark*.
- Closest to book musical.
- An uptempo swing narrative.
- Broadway Kurt Weill, gently ironic and humorous.
- Suitable for a range of auditions: Brecht, sketch shows, situations requiring cabaret style, auditions requesting non musical material and as a contrasting (second) song for mainstream musicals.
- Requires cuts (see Chapter 11).

vi.   '*Worst Pies in London*' from *Sweeney Todd*.
- Verismo musical or melodrama.
- An uptempo point number.
- Strong and dramatic, humorous, requiring very quick changes of thought and excellent comic timing.
- May require cuts.

vii.   '*Could I Leave You?*' from *Follies*.
- Concept musical.
- An uptempo waltz.
- Ironic, biting humour and strength.
- Could be used as a second song for other types of audition.

viii.   '*What Did I Have That I Don't Have?*' from *On a Clear Day*.
- Concept musical.
- Ballad (not many sustained notes).
- A working-out song with humorous undertones.
- Good vehicle for a range of voice qualities including belt notes.

ix.   '*A Trip to the Library*' from *She Loves Me*.
- Classic book.
- A point number for best friend.
- Somewhat ditzy, comic love-song.
- May require cuts.

x.   '*Hold On*' from *The Secret Garden*.
- Concept musical.
- An uptempo point number with several changes of pace.
- Contemporary musical style.
- Pragmatic young character.
- Can be used for verismo auditions as it is strong and direct.
- Can be sung without the second verse.

xi.   '*Take It On the Chin*' from *Me and My Girl*.
- Classic book or musical comedy.
- An uptempo number.
- Putting on a brave face when your world has fallen apart. (This is the most poignant song in the list.)

- Useful for English play with music. Period feel.
- Can be sung without verse.

xii.   '*I Hear Bells*' from *Starting Here Starting Now*.
- Sketch or revue.
- An uptempo number.
- Gently quirky, philosophical and positive.
- Possibility for belt at the end.
- Non-gender-specific.
- A useful second song.
- Can be sung without second verse.

xiii.   '*It Needs Work*' from *City of Angels*.
- Concept musical.
- A swing uptempo number.
- Contemporary jazz style.
- Comedy and ironic.
- Can be cut.

xiv.   '*The Wages of Sin*' from *The Mystery of Edwin Drood*.
- Concept musical but with verismo feel.
- A narrative ballad.
- An excellent all-purpose actor-singer song, useful for a variety of auditions.

xv.   '*Holding to the Ground*' from *Falsettos*.
- Concept musical.
- A dramatic uptempo number.
- An ordinary woman in unexpected circumstances, stoical and humorous.
- Contemporary, but can be used for verismo.
- Can be cut.

xvi.   '*Shy*' from *Once Upon a Mattress*.
- Concept musical.
- An uptempo number.
- Comedy with personality.
- Classic style, and therefore could be used for classic book auditions.

xvii.   '*It's An Art*' from *Working*.
- Concept or sketch musical.
- An uptempo waltz.
- Comedy.
- It can be sung in different styles, ranging from genteel waitress to Madame Thenardier, and it is therefore suitable for a variety of auditions.
- Requires cuts.

xviii.   '*I'm Breaking Down*' from *Falsettos*.
  - Concept musical.
  - A swing uptempo number. Contemporary ragtime.
  - An ironic nervous breakdown song, with very quick changes of thought.
  - Requires cuts.

xix.   '*Cats Are Purrfect*' from *Dick Whittington*.
  An unaccompanied number that was written for her in pantomime.

xx.   '*I Take My Chances*' by Mary-Chapin Carpenter and Don Schlitz.
  - Pop (or folk rock).
  - Rock ballad.
  - Tough, independent, resigned.
  - May need transposing.
  - Useful for musicals auditions that specify a pop number. (For an actor-singer looking for narrative and dramatic content, we advise singer-songwriter material rather than pop diva; consider songs by Amanda McBroom, Vonda Shephard, John Bucchino, Diane Warren, Kirsty McColl, James Taylor, Lennon and McCartney, and Elton John.)

6. Out of the database, these are the songs that were used to make up the portfolio:

i.   '*Moments in the Woods*'. This became her number one song.

ii.   '*The Saga of Jenny*'. This song was chosen because of its suitability for a range of auditions.

iii.   '*But Not For Me*'. This became her standard or book musical song, as well as her lyrical ballad. It was also her versatile speed song. She had it transposed to fit her comfort zone, and it doubled as a back-up song for auditions with poor pianists.

iv.   '*The Wages Of Sin*'. Character tart number.

v.   '*Hold On*'. This song was useful to demonstrate the younger end of her playing range.

vi.   '*Cats Are Purrfect*'. This unaccompanied song showed off her excellent speech quality and some belt.
  We also included a song for a work area specific to actor singers – an English play with music (stage or TV), one song to show one extreme of her playing range, and one general pop number.

vii.   '*Take It On the Chin*'. This was useful for her auditions for plays with incidental singing. '*The Wages of Sin*' is a back-up for this category as the writing is less stylised.

viii.   '*Could I Leave You?*'. This shows the top end of her playing
               range.
xi.   '*I Take My Chances*'. This was her general pop number.
               You can see how many songs from of the sample portfolio
               fitted into the 'unusual circumstances' category and also
               enabled RD to show a range of her dramatic skills. Your
               casting category does not have to be limiting.
7. You will see that over half the original database was put to one
   side. Here's why:
i.   Unsuitable casting or feel: '*What Did I Have That I Don't
               Have?*' (leading lady, although it has potential for a new
               reading), '*A Trip to the Library*' (not intelligent enough),
               and '*It Needs Work*' (wrong physical type, too sassy).
ii.   Unsuitable for her voice type: '*I'm Breaking Down*' (energy
               too nervous and vocally required a finesse that she felt she
               did not yet have).
iii.   Other songs might be kept on the back-burner: '*Worst Pies
               in London*' (this was a part RD could definitely grow into),
               '*Holding to the Ground*' (vocally she didn't feel ready for
               this song as she felt it was a big sing), '*Shy*' (she liked the
               song but felt it needed an audience; she might do it for a
               pantomime audition); similarly with '*Naughty Baby*' (the
               vamp song), '*I Hear Bells*' (she liked the text but felt the
               song was too sustained and needed a more skilled vocalist),
               and '*It's An Art*' (she liked the song but wasn't sure when
               to use it).

Going through this process does mean investing some time (and
money) in research, classes and lessons, and you will find it pays off.
There is no need for the whole portfolio to be in place before you
start working on the songs; this would hardly be practical. As long as
you have done the *FOAL* Interview and know your Profile, you will
be tuned in to looking for songs that will fall into your *FOAL* area.9

Chapter 9

Conscious Learning

Many actors find it difficult to learn songs, even though they are used to learning and memorising substantial amounts of text. How well you learn the song at the start will impact on how effectively you will eventually memorise it. Learning and memorising are not the same thing. The tasks involved in song preparation are: spoken text and meaning (which give you the framework for character), the musical text and style (this includes the learning of rhythm and pitch), and the diction score (the marrying of text with music). In this chapter we will also be discussing the preparation of your musical score: checking your key and getting the song transposed if necessary. All of these items are your responsibility, even if writing out the music is not something you can do yourself. By the end of this chapter you will have prepared your score for rehearsal.

Learning a song is a complex task, requiring you to memorise rhythmic patterns, pitches and words. Often the words are broken down into syllables, or syllables are slurred together in an unexpected way, or unstressed syllables are set on long notes making them appear stressed ... and so on. All of these things can be discouraging to an actor who is used to working with text and the 'flavour' of words. If you do not read music (and many actors do not) then you must find a strategy for learning your song accurately. Breaking the learning process down into smaller tasks will not only cut down your learning time, it will also make it more effective.

Learn a song in fifteen minutes

1. Pick a short song as an exercise, preferably one that you do not know at all. Forget the music to start with, and read the words as a script. This will help you to scan the phrases and get the overall meaning of the song. Put in the natural speech inflections and stresses that you would for a poem or piece of prose. Do not attempt to memorise anything at this stage.
2. Speak the words in the rhythm and the speed of the music. You may need help with this from a coach, singing teacher or a

recorded version of the song (definitely the least favoured option because it contains the nuances of someone else's performance). It is a good idea to beat time (the main pulses in the bar) as you do this, either by clicking you fingers, tapping your foot or clapping. Make sure that you elongate any syllables that are set on long notes or linked together in the music. At this stage you will almost certainly notice that there are some syllables that are now stressed differently; some of them may even go against the natural speech inflection of the word. This is fine; notice it and mark it in your copy for the time being. Here are some examples of what we mean.

This Is the Moment

This IS the   mo - MENT   This IS the   DAY

So Many People

man   FOR   me___   must have a   cast - LE___

Unusual Way

but some - how IT will   ne - -   VER end___

This is also a good time to notice any unusual words or sounds and to pace your breath. The rhythm will dictate a different phrasing and hence will affect your breath use, so you need to be aware of this. Do not attempt to sing the melody at this stage; merely intone the words in the rhythm.

3. Listen to the melody once through without singing at all. Make sure that your pianist or coach plays just the melody and counts out the beats for places where you are not singing. This will help you to get used to scanning the breaks between your entries.

4. Now siren (singing quietly on 'ng') the melody along with the piano or keyboard. The siren should be quiet and small. Do not try

to listen to yourself: the aim of the siren is for you to develop a muscular memory for the pattern of pitches that make up the melody. Sirening can set your voice up for the sustaining of pitch which is a feature of singing, and the effort levels that singing demands; this is different from speech. You will also be far more aware, when sirening, of how to negotiate large or awkward intervals in the song and high or low points in your range.

Repeat this stage as many times as you need until you can do the melody accurately with the piano. If you are in a coaching session or have the full accompaniment on tape, you can repeat the sirening stage with the performance tape at any stage of rehearsal for the song.

5. Mirening[1] is the first stage of putting the words and the melody together. Mirening means to mouth the words at the front of the mouth while keeping the 'ng' hum at the back. The tongue is very agile, and you can separate the actions of the tongue tip, the blade, the sides and the back. Make sure that you articulate all the consonants that are made near the front of the mouth. The only ones that you cannot shape are 'k' and 'g' because you would need to release the 'ng'. You can also separate the action of the lips from the tongue to make the round vowels as in 'AW' (as in law), 'OO' (move), 'o' (hot) and 'oo' (book).

Mirening can also be repeated at later stages of rehearsal and is a good warm-up exercise on the day of your audition.

6. Sing the words and melody together. If you make any errors, repair the relevant phrase immediately without going through the whole song again. You will know the material well enough by now to be able to sing fragments of it accurately. If you are having difficulty pitching a note after a music break, we recommend that you siren to the tune of the music break until you are confident with your entry. At this stage, if the accompaniment is complex, make sure that you understand how to count in all your entries.

Stages 2–6 in our opinion will benefit from being done with a pianist, coach or someone who reads music reliably. If you programme in mistakes at this stage it is very difficult to correct them later. Actors who have taken part in this song-learning process described above report knowing the song better after fifteen to twenty minutes of rehearsal time than songs they had spent weeks learning by themselves.

---

[1]For a more detailed explanation of Mirening see *Singing and The Actor* p 64

Rehearsal tapes

We think rehearsal tapes are a good idea, so that actors can complete the learning and memorising process on their own. Jeremy records at least two versions for this purpose: one with just the melody, one with the accompaniment. Sometimes a third tape is required with the accompaniment slower if the song is fast and complex. It is absolutely fine to have a tape at working or 'thinking' speed when you are still learning the song.

Memorising

Studies of the psychology of learning have shown that, having learned something correctly, singers memorise words better with music than without. This may come as a surprise to the novice singer, but think of how often when a fragment of a song comes into your head you can nearly always recall the words as well as the tune. Conversely, if someone asked you to recite the words of a current pop ballad, you would find it much easier to do if you mentally 'hummed' the melody as you did so. The key thing is to do your learning consciously: you will learn more accurately and faster, and find memorising easier. The learning process we have outlined above is the first step in conscious learning. As you prepare your score for rehearsal you will make decisions about how to articulate the text. This 'diction score' will enable you to develop a muscular memory for your song so that it is more likely to remain embedded when you are under the stress of auditioning. There are further techniques on memorising described in Chapter 10.

YOUR REHEARSAL SCORE

In our workshops with actors on song preparation we will often include a section on making up a 'diction score'. This is really a form of script marking that will ensure you target the words and syllables that you intend in performance and that the listener hears them in real time. One of the problems you may experience with sung text is that you are not in control of the timing of the music. In addition to this you may be asked to concentrate on the vocal line (melody) and to make it continuous. As a result the energy of the consonants can be lost. As a basic rule you can and should work the consonants as hard in sung text as you do in projected speech; the only difference is in the timing. This requires you to make decisions at an early stage of your learning. The diction score will help you in this process. Here are some general points.

1. For maximum (instant) intelligibility, vowels and consonants of a word need to be heard equally well. Unless you rebalance the relationship between them, vowels will be heard as louder than consonants. Consonants are made by obstructing the vocal tract (at the lips, at the tongue and teeth and so on) and are short in duration. Vowels are made with an open or unobstructed vocal tract and are easily sustained.

2. In sung text the melody is created by elongating the vowels. This is a different balance of targets than in spoken voice, and the consonants must be exaggerated even more than in speech if the audience is to hear them. Exaggeration means either doing them louder or for longer.

3. In song, actors often run words and syllables together that they would never do in speech. This may create nonsense words – 'tie-meal-severything' (time heals everything) – and is to be avoided. Using the diction score, both line and intelligibility become possible.

Preparing your rehearsal score

Here's an extract from Stephen Sondheim's '*With So Little To Be Sure Of*' from the musical *Anyone Can Whistle*.

> **With so little to be sure of,**
> **If there's anything at all,**
> **If there's anything at all,**
> **I'm sure of here and now and us together.**

1. Punctuation and syntax will often reveal important things about the text and the thought process of the character. These four lines, set over sixteen bars of music, make up one complete statement. There's a kind of Woody Allen-esque thought qualification in the sub-clauses ('If there's anything at all' said twice with different emphases on 'if' and 'at all'), and this is revealing of many layers beneath what is being said. Pay particular attention to the placement of the commas in the text. Because of the way the melody runs on in between the third and fourth line (overlapping the sense) it would be easy to scan the words thus:

   > **'If there's anything at all I'm sure of'** and then make the new line begin

   > **'Here and now and us together'**, which would give a completely different reading of the text.

2. Note the relationship between the text and the melodic line. Sondheim has said that he doesn't write tunes but if that is the case

then this song (originally a duet) is an exception, with a lovely soaring melodic line that belies the text. This may well have been the composer's intention and so you must give it your attention. Whatever, do not get seduced by the melody. Indeed, the diction score will help you to resolve any difficulties that arise from the setting of the words.

Always work with two copies when learning a new song, one for the pianist and one for you. You may even like to write the words out separately, preferably double-spaced, for your own markings. This becomes part of your working copy.

Making the diction score

We recommend that you do this work soon after your first session on learning the song. This will enable you to target any difficulties of intelligibility at an early stage, to find solutions, and to check that they work with the music.

1. Speak the words out loud slowly, making sure of each syllable. It is easy to distort and make nonsense of a word if you do not target the vowels correctly. Because in singing everything is elongated you will find it helpful to write down all the component sounds of each word.
2. Work out how many sounds are required to make each syllable. You can do this with or without using phonetics. In *Singing and The Actor*[2] this process is described in detail using phonetic analysis, but you do not need to do this every time you learn a song. When you come to count the sounds in each word, mark compound vowels in as '2' or '3'.

    For example, 'Sure' breaks down into 'sh' + 'ou' + 'uh' = 3 (Standard British) or 'sh' + 'ou' + 'rr' (Standard American).

    'An-y-thing' breaks down into 'e' + 'n' + 'EE' + 'th' + 'ih' + 'ng' = 6
3. Now speak the text just sounding the consonants. Notice where you are working to make the consonant, how hard you are working and what is happening with your breath. For example, the breath passes through when you say 'th' of 'with' and the 's' of 'so'; and the breath is stopped when you sing the 't' and 'g' of 'together'.

If you want the check the correct placement of consonants refer to *Singing and The Actor* pp 141–142 or Michael McCallion's *The Voice Book* pp 137–138. Checking the placement of consonants is something you will find really useful if you are having difficulty executing a particular word on a note that you can sing perfectly well on a vowel.

[2]*Singing and The Actor* pp 151-2

4. Underline all the voiced consonants in the text; this will remind you to sing them on pitch.
   So the diction score now reads like this:

W<u>ith</u> so <u>l</u>itt-<u>le</u> to <u>be</u> sure o<u>f</u>,
  3   3   3 2 2 2   3   2

If <u>there's</u> a<u>n</u>-y-thi<u>ng</u> at a<u>ll</u>,
 2   4   2 1   3 2 2

If <u>there's</u> a<u>n</u>-y-thi<u>ng</u> at a<u>ll</u>,
 2   4   2 1   3 2 2

I'<u>m</u> sure o<u>f</u> here a<u>nd</u> <u>n</u>ow a<u>nd</u> us to-ge-<u>th</u>er.
 3   3   2   3   3   3   3 2 2 2 2

Key: underlining indicates voiced consonants.
(In standard US, the 'th' of with is unvoiced.)

---

5. At this point you can make a decision about whether to sing the song with American or English vowels; that can depend on the audition you are doing. If, for example, you were auditioning for the role of Hapgood and had been asked to learn this number, then you would do it in American. Likewise, if you had been asked to audition for a specifically American show such as *Chicago*. The key thing is to avoid singing vowels that are not there just because you are singing.
6. Now speak the text aloud again, this time in the rhythm of the music, just as you did in stage 2 of the song learning process. Notice how the timing of the music requires you to make certain adjustments. When you come to sing the text this becomes more marked because you have to add pitch.

Adjustments

i. Notice what happens to short vowels (such as 'w<u>i</u>th') when sung on a long note; check that you are still singing the right vowel if a short vowel is set on a long note.
ii. Make sure that you sing all the sounds in compound vowels. If you have two vowels to sing on a long note, make a decision about where the second vowel is to come in. You can discuss this with your vocal coach or the musical director.

iii. When you have a voiced consonant, sing it on the pitch of the note. This is especially useful in sung text because it gives you space for the consonant in the time-frame of the note and ensures that you avoid scooping.

iv. Make time in the music for the unvoiced consonants. This is something that the composer assumes you are going to do but he or she doesn't write it in. As a general rule, you must rob time from the written music in order to make time for the consonants.

    a. If a consonant is at the beginning of a word, you must make it *before* the written note, so that you arrive on the vowel in time;

    b. If it is in the middle or at the end of a word, you must rob time from the note itself to make the consonant, otherwise you are in danger of attaching it to the beginning of the next word or syllable.

When marking your working copy you might like to indicate this by writing the consonant in where it is actually made.

v. Avoid running words into each other, making nonsense words. This can happen when a new word begins with a vowel: see example B below. Separate the vowel from the preceding consonant by making a new onset into the vowel. For a description of onsets see *Singing and The Actor* pages 16–18. In this instance you would use a glottal onset which can be indicated on your score by the apostrophe (').

With So Little To Be Sure Of

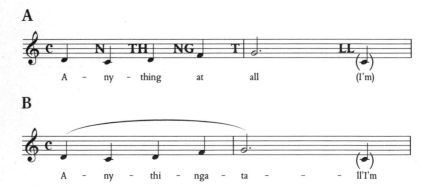

vi. Avoid making extra vowels between words. This can happen between words that end and begin with consonants as well as between vowels and consonants. As a general rule you can avoid this if you focus on the words rather than on the vocal line. Remember that with unvoiced consonants you are not singing as you make them, you only sing *after or before* them. If you try to sing through them, you are likely to change the consonant and thus the meaning to make these extra vowels.

Here's a complete diction score of the first sixteen bars of '*With So Little To Be Sure Of*'. We have marked in all the voiced consonants, indicated where vowels should be separated from the previous word, and where the voice must be stopped after stopped consonants to avoid extra vowels that are not in the text.

W<u>ith</u>/so <u>l</u>itt-<u>l</u>e to <u>be</u> <u>s</u>ure 'o<u>f</u>,
3   3   3 2 2 2   3   2

'If/<u>there</u>'s /a<u>n</u>-y-thi<u>ng</u>/at/a<u>ll</u>,
2 4   2 1   3 2 2

'If/<u>there</u>'<u>s</u> 'a<u>n</u>-y-thi<u>ng</u> 'at 'a<u>ll</u>,
2 4   2 1   3 2 2

'I'<u>m</u> sure 'o<u>f</u>/here 'a<u>nd</u>/<u>n</u>ow/ 'a<u>nd</u>/ 'u<u>s</u>/ to-ge-<u>ther</u>
 3 3   2   3   3   3   3   2 2 2 2

Key: underlining indicates voiced consonants. The ' indicates
a glottal onset.
/ Indicates a watchpoint where you need to avoid making extra vowels
between words or avoid running them together.

Note that lines 2 and 3 are interpreted differently. By moving the glottals, you get a different reading.

You will see that in working this process we have moved from working with spoken text to sung text. You will probably want to run past your coach or singing teacher any adjustments that have to be made to make the text work with the music. When you are happy with these decisions, write them into your working copy of the music. This copy will then form the basis of your rehearsal process.

PREPARING YOUR MUSIC SCORE
Checking your key

Making sure that you have the song in the right key is essential. There is nothing more embarrassing than turning up at the audition and hearing your song played in a different key. In these cases the key is nearly always higher than the one you have rehearsed, which makes for vocal difficulties as well. There are two aspects to checking your key:

1. Are you are singing in the same key as your sheet music?
2. Is the song in a suitable key for you?

If you do not read music then it is easy to come adrift somewhere between these two factors. Let's examine more closely what they mean.

When we talk about 'your key' we are using it in the sense of range and comfort zone (see Chapter 3). Ideally a song should be within your comfort zone on the whole, with one or two notes above or below and not out of your range. Never take a song to an audition that is out of your range. You will know after a few runs through of the song, whether or not it fits into the category of 'your key'.

Your sheet music

Whatever you take to the audition for the pianist to play must be in the key that you are used to singing and must be written out in that key. To take the music in the wrong key tends to show that you are ill-prepared. Just think how you would feel if you had to sightread eighty different scenes a day and were asked to read one text in a different language on spec. You cannot expect the pianist to give you his or her best under such conditions. There are some pop auditions where it is acceptable to take a lead sheet and ask to have it played in your key, but we advise always checking this out before you get into the audition.

Sometimes an actor will find a song that they like and rehearse it with a recording. This is fine; just make sure when you have your coaching session that the music you buy is in the same key. Quite often compilations of musicals (rather than the original vocal score with piano reduction) will have some of the songs in different keys. This is done for commercial reasons: if there are a lot of leger lines (the little lines above or below the main stave) or the song is in an awkward key, the publishers will print it in another key, saving on printing costs. Historically, music was commercially more viable to the general public when amateur singers were able to play and sing it for themselves. So do watch out for these easy piano versions: they are wonderful for the general public but might ruin your audition!

Transposing your song

There are two situations in which you might want to get your song transposed:

1. When you know that the cast recording of your chosen song is in a different key and if that is the key you want to sing in, get the song transposed. If the song is not published in the right key, you might be able to get a copy of it from someone who has been in the cast.

2. When you have found a song that you really like but it is either out of your range or doesn't read well in the published key. By 'read well' we mean that you lose the 'feel' of the song when it is in the higher or lower (more rare) key. Typical examples of the latter are the Gershwin songs published in the compilation albums. These keys do not work for most female voices as they are generally high and tend to make the singer sound too operatic. As a general rule is it OK to get standards transposed into a key that suits you. The same is true of most of the pop repertoire.

Some musical directors that we interviewed for the final section of the book indicated that they weren't really bothered if a song was transposed from its original key. As far as they were concerned, if the performance worked that was far more important than the key. However, here are a few situations in which that might not apply and when we think you should avoid taking a song that has been transposed.

1. When you are taking a song from the show that you are auditioning for. Generally we do not advise doing this anyway for auditions. Taking a song from the show that you are up for tells the panel that you think you are suitable for a particular role; you had better be extremely sure of yourself if this is the case. An additional factor to be aware of is that the panel is less likely to consider you for other parts in the show, since you are clearly targeting a particular role. If a song that you like feels way out of your range, then it means it is not for your voice type. The composer wrote the song in that key because he had a particular vocal characterisation in mind and you will be changing the casting category if you transpose the song into another key. Some of the long running commercial shows do make allowances in this respect for cast changes, and may have even versions of the same song in more than one key, but do not depend on it. If you think of the logistics of having all the band parts written out in several keys, then you will realise why the original is the best.

2. When the song you have chosen has a particular 'money note' in it that you cannot do (for example the high G# sung by Phantom in Andrew Lloyd Webber's *'Music Of The Night'*). The money note is there for a reason, and the panel will know that the reason why you

have transposed the song is because you can't do it. Remember that the point of the audition is to show what you *can* do. (A money note is one that raises the vocal excitement factor in a song and becomes one that – literally – audiences will pay good money to hear.)

When you do get your song transposed there are one or two guidelines to follow.

1. If you are fortunate enough to be able to do the work yourself, make sure that the manuscript is legible. An important factor for the audition pianist will be that the words are clearly written out and underneath the notes they are sung on. Do not assume that because you know the words, the pianist only needs to concern him/herself with the notes. A good pianist will be reading all three lines of music *and* taking in the words.
2. If you are have been asked specifically to bring a pop song or jazz standard, then it will be sufficient to bring your transposition lead sheet style: that is with the melody and words written out and the accompaniment in chord symbols. If you are taking a song of this type to a mainstream musical theatre audition, you cannot rely on the pianist being a great sight-reader as well as an improviser and we recommend that you get the piano part written out.

A word of warning about pop songs. Though you may be able to buy these in the original key in the sheet music, the piano rendition may bear little resemblance to the sound track you are used to hearing. Rather like the easy piano version, the publishers often leave out parts of the backing when publishing the song: it is not uncommon for there to be a bass line with a few chords filled in and the right hand simply following the voice line. A good pianist will instinctively try to give you more, but for an audition you need to give him or her as much help as you can. When you rehearse the song with your coach, get them to put in any musical directions they think necessary for the audition pianist to be able to realise the accompaniment with style. If your vocal coach or singing teacher doesn't know the song, take a recording of it into your session, so that they can get the right feel for the backing.

Conscious learning in summary

What's the time scale for doing all of this? We began this chapter by talking about 'conscious learning', that is a process by which you can make sure that your material is properly prepared. All performers have some kind of a learning process whether conscious or instinctive. You have two scripts to learn when you are working on a song, so the process is really important. Here is a suggested schedule for the process:

1. Learn a song in fifteen minutes. This really *does* mean fifteen minutes! This should be done at the first music session or singing lesson that you have on the song. Record the whole session on tape or minidisc.

2. Diction score. Preliminary work on this could be done before the fifteen minute song learning. Having learned the rhythms and set the pulse, however, you will want to make adjustments to the diction score after or during the song-learning session. Make a special note of any sounds that you find difficult to execute on certain notes.

3. Prepare your rehearsal score at this point. Remember that the pianist will need another clean score, with his markings for the audition (see Chapter 13).

4. Your key. The first learning session will establish whether or not you can do the song in the written key. Discuss and try out alternatives with your coach or singing teacher. Most pianists will be able to ghost a transposition for you or, failing that, start you off on the right note so that you can try it out a cappella. Record this session so that you can rehearse in the new key to check that it really does work for you.

5. Auditions have a habit of turning up when least expected: if you are planning to sing the song in the near future get it transposed by someone reliable. Expect to pay for this service unless a friend does it as a favour. Make sure that the transposition is clearly and neatly done if it is handwritten and get it checked before you go to the audition. Do not take the song to audition unless you have had it transposed. A lead sheet will do for some pop auditions; always write out the words under each verse.

6. Cuts. Learn the whole song first, even if there are a lot of verses, and sort out your cuts when you are about to start the memorising process. Memorising will be discussed in Chapter 12 and cuts in Chapter 11.

7. Practise your song with a pianist some time before taking it to an audition. It's a great opportunity to find out if you really know the song well, and you will be working with someone who may not have seen your music score before. If the accompaniment bears no resemblance to what you are expecting, it's better to find out in the safe haven of a coaching studio. Make the most of each opportunity to show what you can do at your audition.

Chapter 10

Making Decisions

Preparing a song for audition requires you to make a number of decisions. Some of these are decisions that you make as an actor whenever you prepare a new piece of text, or that you make during the course of rehearsal. Others are decisions that you might make specifically for an audition situation. In particular you will find that decisions about focus or 'playing the song' may well change when you are performing the song at audition.

Function

You must understand the context of a song and know its function within its show. By using the 'Five W's' – Who? Why? What? Where? When? – you will be able to flesh out the details of the song. In addition to its function within the whole show, every song will have its own function (the answer to the question Why?), and this will give you the 'song journey'. Let's go through the Five W's process for the song '*Moments in the Woods*' from Stephen Sondheim's *Into The Woods*. This is a song for female voice, soprano or mezzo. It's performed by a lead in the show, and the casting could be for character actress or best friend type.

1. Who are you?

   You are the baker's wife, between twenty-eight and forty years old, married and childless due to a curse on your husband's family by the witch, desperate to have children, peasant class and hard-working.

2. Why are you singing the song? (What do you want to achieve by the end of it? How is that a useful stepping stone in the larger context of the musical?)

   You want to work something out for yourself. You have just had a fling with Cinderella's prince. You are a married woman and, he is of much higher status than you. You enjoyed the fling, but it was fleeting, and you need to make sense of it. In the context of the musical this is one of many scenes in which a character finds him/herself in an unusual situation. It enables the audience get an insight into how life can change at any moment and that

this can be an opportunity for growth.
3. Where are you when you sing the song?
    You are in a glade in the woods. The situation is private.
4. When are you singing the song? What has happened just before? What follows the song?
    The baker's wife has just had her interlude with Cinderella's prince. His last words were, 'I shall not forget you, how brave you are to be alone in the woods. And how alive you've made me feel.' He then leaves. He has made it clear that their liaison has just been a 'moment' and should be enjoyed for just that. Immediately following the song the footsteps of the giantess are heard as she seeks revenge for the death of her husband.
5. What exactly are you saying in the song?
    Like all good fairy tales the story of *Into The Woods* can be received on many levels, and it is up to the audience what they make of it. As an auditionee, it's important that you are aware of the layers beneath the words. As we examine what the baker's wife is saying in the song, some of these levels will be revealed.
    Here is the complete text [with suggested subtext].

    i. **What was that?** (spoken)
       Was that me? (sung from here onwards)
       Was that him?
       Did a prince really kiss me?
       And kiss me?
       And kiss me?
       And did I kiss him back? [Wow! Did that really happen with *him?* Did I really do *that?*]

    ii. **Was it wrong?**
        Am I mad?
        Is that all?
        Does he miss me?
        Was he suddenly getting bored with me? [That's not like me. Is it going to happen again? Why did it stop? Did I do something wrong?]

    iii. **Wake up!**
         Stop dreaming.
         Stop prancing about the woods.
         It's not beseeming.
         What is it about the woods?

    iv. **Back to life,**
        Back to sense,
        Back to child,
        Back to husband,

No-one lives in the woods.
There are vows,
There are needs,
There are ties,
There are standards,
There are shouldn'ts and shoulds. [Let's be sensible about this.
I am not in reality; no-one runs their life like that.]

v.   Why not both instead?
There's the answer, if you're clever:
Have a child for warmth,
And a baker for bread and a prince for whatever. [After all,
why not?]
Never! It's these woods. [I can't believe I said that!]

vi. Face the facts, find the boy,
Join the group, stop the giant,
Just get out of these woods. [Be realistic. What was I doing
before I came in? This is dangerous.]

vii. Was that him?
Yes it was.
Was that me?
No, it wasn't,
Just a trick of the woods. [That feeling's come back again; I
mustn't give in to it.]

viii. Just a moment,
One peculiar passing moment, [Ahhh, it was *good!*]
Must it all be either less or more,
Either plain or grand?
Is it always 'Or'?
Is it never 'And'? [Do I have to choose?]
That's what woods are for: [Yes...]
For those moments in the woods. [Because it's good to have
choices!]

ix. Oh, if life were made of moments, [Wouldn't it be nice if...]
Even now and then a bad one!
But if life were only moments,
Then you'd never know you had one. [I like the stable things
in my life and something changing brings this into focus.]

x.   First a witch, then a child,
Then a prince, then a moment --
Who can live in these woods? [I thought I knew what I wanted
from life.]
And to get what you wish,
Only just for a moment --

> **These are dangerous woods...** [Now I'm not so sure.]
>
> xi. **Let the moment go...**
> **Don't forget it for a moment, though.** [I realise I can't hang onto things.]
> **Just remembering you've had an 'And' when you're back to 'Or'**
> **Makes the 'Or' mean more than it did before.** [The experience has enriched me.]
> **Now I understand --** [and I am OK with it!]
> **And it's time to leave the woods!**

Sondheim writes wonderful lyrics that enable you to find a lot of the subtext just from careful reading. What you won't get, if you have not studied the song's larger context, is the reference to the baker and his wife seeking help from the witch to their problem of childlessness, itself a result of a curse cast by the witch on the baker's family. Nor would you know about the effect that the angry widowed giantess is having on the whole community.

Whenever you are working on a new song, write out the text with a subtext in your own words alongside it. Then mark in the main changes of thought that will become landmarks on the song's journey. Remember that by the end of the song something must have changed or there would be no reason for you to sing it.

Focus

This is a word that can have many meanings, particularly in an acting context. We mean specifically 'to whom you are singing'. In his book *On Singing on Stage*, David Craig defines three types of focus: Unifocus, House number, and Internalised focus. We will use these categories as our starting point. This will enable you to make decisions about how you can play the song in an audition situation.

Unifocus songs. These are directed to a specific 'you'. On stage you would either be singing to that person or singing about them. In an audition that person is still present to the degree that we can see his or her effect on you while you are singing. Example songs include '*Send In the Clowns*' from *A Little Night Music* (where the object of the song is present), '*Out of My Dreams*' from *Oklahoma!* (where he is not), and '*God on High*' from *Les Misérables* (where he is not – at least visibly – present), and '*Look What Happened to Mabel*' from *Mack and Mabel* (where the singer is singing to herself as another person).

Some unifocus songs are directed to a plural you as in the American sense of 'you-all'. '*Use What You Got*' from *The Life* would be an example.

House numbers. These are directed to everyone present and across the fourth wall. In this sense you could say that the audience becomes part of the cast during a house number. Example songs include '*If You Want to Die in Bed*' from *Miss Saigon*, '*Master of the House*' from *Les Misérables* and '*Comedy Tonight*' from *A Funny Thing Happened on the Way to the Forum*.

Internalised focus songs. These are soliloquies in the true sense of the word. The performer addresses the lyrics to himself and is usually working out some kind of a problem. Examples include '*What am I Doin'?*' from *Closer Than Ever*, and '*Where am I Going?*' from *Sweet Charity*. '*Moments in the Woods*' also falls into this category.

Decisions about voice quality

Voice qualities are wonderful interpretative tools. Having worked through the process of preparation in Chapter 9 you will now be ready to make decisions about voice quality.

1. Whatever voice qualities you choose, you must sound like the character. You will want to avoid pop idioms that are sound and not character-driven.
2. You need to make decisions about the general characteristics of the baker's wife: her age, status, physical attributes and so on. This will give you an idea of what she will sound like generally. Sondheim has done most of this work for you in his musical writing.
3. For specifics, you must look at what you are saying and why. This brings us back to the song journey. Here are some suggested voice qualities for the first twenty-four bars of the song (counting from 'what was that?').

   What was that? You are totally amazed. (Use breathy Speech: it's sensual and strong.)

   Was that me? Unsure and questioning (Falsetto). Take this up until **Did a prince really kiss me?** An emotional memory. Change on 'prince' to something more warm and inviting (Cry).

   And kiss me? And kiss me? Hold in your mind a different place for each kiss. Depending on where it was, your voice quality will change.

   And did I kiss him back? Horrified amazement (Speech. If you want to keep the breathless feel, let a bit of air into the sound without pushing.)

   Was it wrong? Unsure again (Falsetto).

   Am I mad? Self admonitory (Speech).

Is that all? Mad with him now (Speech with Twang).
Does he miss me? Insecure, slightly petulant (Cry).
Was he suddenly getting bored with me? Even more so (take it into Twang).
Wake up! Stop dreaming. Stop prancing about the woods. Pulling yourself up short. Notice the imperatives (Speech and Twang).
It's not beseeming. What is it about the woods? Talking to yourself like a teacher (Speech and Twang, Breathy Speech).

Moments in the Woods

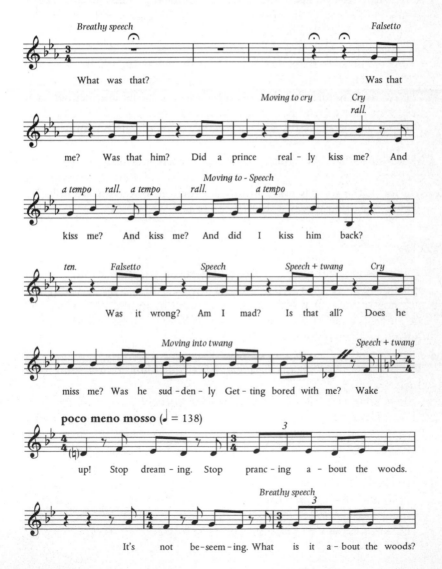

Style

You now know the four elements of style.

1. Show type. *Into the Woods* is a concept show. '*Moments in the Woods*' is a strong acting piece and so would be suitable for concept and sketch shows requiring singer-actor skills. It is probably not suitable for verismo nor classic book auditions.
2. Song type. This is a narrative, discursive song and lies within the point number category. You could not call it a ballad.
3. Musical style. This is undeniably Sondheim, which may make it unsuitable for contemporary musicals by e.g. Frank Wildhorn, Andrew Lloyd Webber in pop mode, or Disney.
4. Vocal style. This is a point number and so should be performed mostly in speech quality and falsetto: the voice qualities of the vernacular. Cry quality might be used for emotional memory and reflection. Remember that twang always 'ups the ante' either as a mix or on its own because it is bright and perceptually louder. This is not a song that calls for belt, neither dramatically nor musically.

Make sure that the song you have chosen enables the panel to envisage you performing in the style of the show they are auditioning you for. If the song is not appropriate for the show you are unlikely to get a recall, however well you perform it.

Play

Doing a song within the context of a show when there are (often) other people on stage is one thing. How do you convey not only the meaning of the words but also their context in an audition situation? We end this chapter with two songs that have complex storylines and that move their points of focus.

'*Vanilla Ice Cream*' from *She Loves Me* by Sheldon Harnick and Jerry Bock.

This song is available in *The Singers Musical Theatre Anthology Soprano Vol. II* (pub. Hal Leonard Corp.). It has been recorded by Barbara Cook (a stunning version), now on CD: *The Broadway Years* Koch 3-7905-2.

(Spoken) 'Dear Friend,'
(Sung) I am so sorry about last night,
It was a nightmare in ev'ry way.
But together, you and I will laugh at last night some day.

Ice cream.

He brought me ice cream.

Vanilla ice cream, imagine that.

Ice cream, and for the first time we were together without a spat.

Friendly, he was so friendly, that isn't like him.

I'm simply stunned.

Will wonders never cease?

Will wonders never cease?

It's been a most peculiar day.

Will wonders never cease? Will wonders never cease?

(Spoken) 'Where was I?'

(Sung very rapidly) 'I am so sorry about last night. It was a nightmare in ev'ry way.

But together you and I will laugh at last night some day.'

I sat there waiting in that café,

And never guessing that you were fat.

That you were near.

You were outside looking bald.

(Spoken) 'Oh, my. Dear Friend.'

(Sung) I am so sorry about last night.

Last night I was so nasty.

Well, he deserved it.

But even so,

That Georg is not like this Georg.

This is a new Georg that I don't know.

Somehow it all reminds me of Dr. Jekyll and Mr. Hyde.

For right before my eyes,

A man that I despise,

Has turned into a man I like.

It's almost like a dream.

And strange as it may seem,

He came to offer me

Vanilla ice cream.

This is a delightful comic song for a lyric soprano. The tessitura is high with a money note at the end (high B), but good speech quality is needed in the lower range as well. Many sopranos like to sing this song because of its combination of comedy and lyric singing. However, out of context the situation is complex to portray:

Amalia, a girl who works in a perfume shop, has been writing to a man she likes but has never met (Dear Friend). They decide to meet at a café one evening. While she is waiting there she sees a man, who she thinks might be the man she is to meet. He is fat and bald. The assignation does not take place because she catches sight of one of her colleagues, Georg, whom she actively dislikes. She is rude to him and leaves out of embarrassment. What she doesn't know is that Georg is Dear Friend. The next day she cries off work with a cold and Georg, inexplicably, appears to comfort her with a gift of vanilla ice cream. For once they do not fight but have a pleasant time together. The song begins as Amalia settles down to write to the 'Dear Friend' about their abortive meeting.

How do you convey this complex situation in an audition? By using musical cues, keywords, and by positioning all the characters you will find that you can convey the context of the song even to a listener who has never seen the show.

Musical cues

Look at the musical structure of the song first. It is unusual in that it has a double verse. In the verse sections, Amalia sings about Dear Friend and in the more sung 'refrain' she is singing about Georg. The rhythmic structure and the orchestration are both very different in each of these sections. We will call these sections A and B. The flavour of them is also different: section A is like notated speech and section B is made up of short excited melodic phrases that build. These differences are important musical cues for the audience.

Focus

The song is an unusual one in that it has more than one focus. The character is on stage alone which makes it a soliloquy. However, at times she is speaking directly to another person (Dear Friend) which makes it unifocus. At other times she is thinking aloud which makes it also internalised focus. The conceit of the song is that it takes time for the audience to find out which man Amalia is talking about. If you can trust this, having worked out who she actually *is* talking about beforehand, you can mirror her own confusion. Amalia's confusion is that:

1. She is falling in love with Georg and doesn't realise it until the end of the song.
2. She does not know that Dear Friend is Georg, and not the fat bald man in the café. (This particular confusion is not resolved until later in the story.)

Positioning and keywords

A good way to practise this song is to have five positions: P1 for you now, P2 for your thoughts about Dear Friend, P3 for your thoughts about Georg earlier today, P4 for your thoughts on Georg at the shop (usually), and P5 for you last night with Dear Friend and Georg. Use as much space as you like to begin with, using diagonals for P1 and 2. Later you can make the change of position much smaller or simply move your eye focus to show the direction of your thoughts.

1. Begin the song in P2, addressing Dear Friend. You are either writing as you speak (sing) or reading out what you have just written.

2. The first change of direction is after the line 'last night some day'. *Do not slow down during this line*; let the audience be surprised when they hear the word 'ice cream'.

3. Use the pause in the music to think about 'ice cream'. You can take your time getting into the next position (P1) because the music starts slowly and builds. 'Ice cream' are keywords in defining a change of focus in the song.

4. Maintain your focus on the joy of the ice cream, until 'imagine that'. Then on 'and for the first time' think of Georg, the pleasure of his visit and that he came bearing a gift. Your manner towards Dear Friend and towards Georg (who brought you ice cream) is different; that is the first clue the audience gets that they may not be the same person. Notice the number of comments or asides you are making throughout this section (whereas when you were starting to write the letter you were speaking directly to Dear Friend).

5. 'Friendly, he was so friendly' refers to P3, Georg earlier today.

6. After you have sung the final 'will wonders never cease?', bring yourself up short and get back to the letter to Dear Friend 'where was I?'. You are almost back in P2.

7. 'I sat there waiting' is back in P2 with Dear Friend. (Back to music A) Without knowing it, Amalia is subconsciously comparing the man she saw at the café, 'fat' and 'bald' with Georg, whom she has just seen. The words fat and bald must take *you* by surprise. Substitute 'near' and 'in' in your head; it will be much funnier!

8. Make sure that the words 'oh, my' are an interjection, not 'oh, my dear friend'. Look to P1 for 'oh, my'. These words are key to the end of the song, for at this point Amalia realises that she cannot consider Dear Friend romantically. And when she sings the words 'I am so sorry about last night' they should be sung in P2, faster (as indicated in the score) and with a firm intention. From this moment on Dear Friend is out of the picture.

9. You are now focussed on Georg, and what happened with him last night (P5). Use P3 (earlier today) and P4 (usually) as you

discuss the relative merits of the different Georgs.

10. The turning point for the end of the song is in the words 'turned into a man I like'. Bring him to P1! Once she has made this admission, Amalia can allow herself to realise that she is in love with someone she already knows, which is why she shrieks with excitement on the words 'ice cream'.

These suggestions about positioning are not intended to be taken as a way of blocking the song, though you might well use them as a basis for doing so if that is your choice. The whole point is to find a way of unravelling the story so that you can reveal it to the audience or panel. Moving through the positions can help you to focus on this.

'What am I doin'?', from *Closer Than Ever* by Richard Maltby Jnr. and David Shire.

This song can be found in the full vocal score of *Closer Than Ever* (pub. Fiddleback Music for Tommy Valando). You can hear it on the original cast recording: RCA Victor 60399-4-RG.

> She was such an incredible woman.
> And one night we both set ourselves free.
> I could feel all the power inside her.
> And she seemed to release it to me.
> Then she suddenly said I can't see her.
> And the thought of it drove me insane.
> So I find up a tree I am creeping,
> To the roof over where she is sleeping,
> And I sit there all night in the rain.
> And I'm thinkin':
> What am I doin' up on a roof?
> What am I doin' out in the rain?
> What kind of feelings make a man blind?
> What am I doin' out of my mind with love?
> (Spoken) And *her* father and *my* father are down on the lawn,
> And they're shouting:
> (Sung) What is he doin' up on a roof?
> What is he doin' out in the rain?
> What kind of feelings make a man blind?
> What kind of guy goes out of his mind with love?
> I decided that I've learned my lesson.
> I rejoined all the sensible men.
> Now no matter how tempting the woman,

I won't ever go crazy again.
When I'm safe and alone in my bedroom,
Thanking God I'm not shaking and wet,
I think back to the night I felt tingles,
Holding tight not to slide down the shingles,
Feeling feelings I'll never forget.
And I wish I was saying:
What am I doin' up on a roof?
What am I doin' out in the rain?
What kind of feelings make a man blind?
What am I doin' out of my mind with...
What am I doin' tailin' her car?
What am I doin' inside her bushes?
What am I doin' covered with mud?
What am I doin' out of my mind with love?
With love?
What am I doin'?
What am I doin' stealin' her scarf?
What am I doin' sniffin' her perfume?
What am I doin' siftin' her trash?
What am I doin' testing her doorknob,
Diallin' her phone,
Tramplin' her tulips,
Buggin' her friends,
Pettin' her dog?
Oh, what am I doin' out of my mind with love?
What am I doin' out of my mind with love?

This is a powerful and passionate song for a dramatic male voice, ranging from C below Middle C to a belted top A, tessitura middle high (baritone). *Closer Than Ever* is in the sketch show category.

This is another complicated song to put across, although there is no through-story in the show, and therefore no show context to set it in. Even though there is no context, you still have to make decisions on the Who? What? When? Where? Why? questions.

There are seven characters: her, me with her (earliest), me on the roof after the break-up (slightly later), me having decided not to get involved (later still but still not in the present), me both here as narrator and in my bedroom (now), her father and my father. One key point is the use of tense – past and present – to denote what is real, what was real then, and what might happen. This can be used as an emotional trigger; he gets more emotionally involved whenever he sings in the present tense. Note that he sings in the present tense as himself both past and present, and also as his own father and her father. However, he doesn't sing as her; he only narrates.

Musical cues

The accompaniment at the beginning of the song is both reflective and rhythmic, with a sustained tune in the right hand and a gently swung rhythm in the left. This left hand figure keeps the song from becoming self-indulgent musically. The vocal line is almost all triplets, contributing to the reflective feel; make the most of them, as they don't appear in the faster section at all. There are subtle changes in the accompaniment that underline the changes of character and timeline. When she says he can't see her, the tune goes into octaves. When he finds himself creeping up a tree, there are arpeggio chords, giving more of a sense of movement and urgency. When he thinks 'What am I doin'?' the feel of the music changes completely: the tempo doubles, the rhythm changes to straight repeated chords, the left hand plays arhythmic octaves, and the chords don't change on the main beats, all of which give the music a driven and off-kilter feel. When he talks about his father and her father the arhythmic left hand and the repeated chords disappear until they shout 'What is he doin'?'

Back as narrator on 'I decided' we are back with the reflective music, although the right hand has thicker chords played more frequently (showing a change of mood from the first time). On 'And I wish I was saying' there is a repeat of the faster feel; although he says he won't ever go there again, the music is almost identical, showing that he longs to feel those feelings again.

Focus

In terms of focus, even though there are seven characters, you really only need three positions: P1 is when he is in the present as himself and narrating; P2 is him with her (where the story begins); P3 is him climbing onto her roof, and this happens the moment he goes into the present tense ('so I find up a tree I am creeping'). This would be a good moment to move physically in an audition as you are referring to what you are doing, for even though you are referring to something you actually did in the past, for you it is real now. While you are now in P3, your father and her father can be standing in P1 (where all the sensible men are). On 'I decided that I've learned my lesson', rejoin the fathers in P1. On 'I think back to the night' refer to P3 and the strong emotions you had never felt until then, and have never felt again; they're very attractive and seductive. The rest of the song can be done from P1, but with a longing for P3 and the man you were then.

Summary

Our aim is for you to come out of the audition knowing that you gave the best performance that you could that day. Every audition is different and you will always be nervous. You will only feel safe in the audition arena if you are able to inhabit your song moment by moment. Making decisions in advance about Style and Play help you to do this. Be as committed and truthful to those decisions in the moment of performance as you can be. Whatever else happens at the audition, your authenticity will show through, enabling the panel to get a good idea of you as a creative artist. You cannot ask for more.

Chapter 11

Making Cuts

There are many situations in which you will need to make cuts in your song. We recommend that you start by learning the whole song: the time to make decisions about cuts is early on in the *memorising* process. Why cut? Some songs are just too long for an audition situation. It is also a truism that the panel will know within bars whether or not you can sing and are the right standard for the place they are looking to fill. The average private audition (first call) lasts between seven-and-a-half and ten minutes, the average open call is five minutes long, and at the end of the spectrum there is the 'show-what-you-can-do-in-sixteen-bars' audition (you could be in and out in three minutes!). Usually, when the panel want to see something more of what you can do, they will direct you to do the song in a different style or with a different motivation, or ask you to sing something else from your portfolio. All of these are good reasons why less is more when we are talking about length of song. Songs are longer than speeches because they have the extra dimension of music, which will include play-ins and play-outs. A song should be no longer than three minutes for a first audition. For open audition calls, prepare short songs (one to two minutes maximum) or song extracts, and always have a sixteen bar unit ready just in case.

A performable unit

Just as with audition speeches, making a performable unit is the key to cutting your song. The scenario or song journey needs to be clear and it has to work musically. Although you may be attached to a particular section of the song (because it shows this or that aspect of your vocal or dramatic skill) cut it if you know the song is too long. You do not need to show everything you can do in the audition, however tempting that may be. Remember that the aim is to give the panel a clear message about you and your skills.

Sometimes you are asked when you arrive at an audition to sing a cut version of your song. It is always worthwhile knowing how long your song actually lasts – duration and number of bars – so

108

that if you find yourself in this position *you* get to choose where to start and finish. Some actors we have worked with have reported that they have been allowed to sing the complete song (instead of having to cut it) when they were able to say exactly how many bars it contained. In extreme cases in the UK you are asked to sing (your best) sixteen bars. In the US at some audition calls it is expected that both your piece and your song should fit into one-and-a-half minutes, and the audition usher sits with a stopwatch and a gong! Managements in this country have been known to ask the usher to stand by the piano and count the bars while they are being sung. Remember that the purpose of a 'sixteen bar' audition is to demonstrate that you can sing in tune, are comfortable with sung text, and to show some of your vocal personality. If you don't want to risk your money notes in those circumstances, choose a section that shows your ability with sung text; perhaps your descriptive talents are demonstrated better in the 'recitative' section of a song. If you are attending an open call, we recommend that you arrive armed with two cut versions: one medium length and one sixteen bars long. Make sure that you are used to performing the song in each cut version.

HOW TO MAKE YOUR CUTS

In order to help you identify what is a performable unit, you will need to consider the musical structure of the song. If you don't read music then you may need some help with this from either your singing coach or a friend who plays keyboard. For the purposes of this chapter we are going to discuss the characteristics of three broad categories of song and how they might be successfully cut.

Simple verse-chorus songs

Many standards and songs by the Gershwin brothers, Irving Berlin, Cole Porter, and Rodgers and Hart fall into this group. Typically these songs will begin with a verse (usually short) and move into a chorus, which may appear once or twice. Examples would be '*My Funny Valentine*' (Rodgers and Hart), '*Our Love Is Here To Stay*' (George and Ira Gershwin), '*Isn't This a Lovely Day?*' (Irving Berlin) and '*I Get a Kick Out of You*' (Cole Porter). Many of these songs are written in sixteen bar units, so if you are looking for sixteen bars, the last sixteen bars of the chorus are a good place to start. If you need more leeway than this (twenty to twenty-four bars for instance) you might want to do a verse and the chorus. Some songs in this category have additional verses (*'They All Laughed'* and *'But Not For Me'* by the Gershwins, *'My Heart Belongs To Daddy'* by Cole Porter, *'Isn't It Romantic?'* by Rodgers and Hart). You don't have to do verse one and chorus one: do the words that you like and can perform best.

Pop songs are included in the verse-chorus category because they are mostly constructed in the same way. There is nearly always a verse-chorus structure in a pop song, even if they do not appear in that order. Many pop songs are constructed in eight and sixteen bar units, making them easy to cut. Narrative pop songs (e.g. *'I will survive'*) will have more than one verse which carries the story, and it is usually longer than those of the 'standards'. The chorus may well appear after each verse and you can then cut back to another verse, omitting some of the repetition. Watch out for instrumental breaks that are used to 'build' in the commercial recordings but do nothing for you in audition circumstances; cut them out. Often a pop song will have the final chorus in a higher key or with a different ending so you must pay attention to this if you want to convey that excitement factor in your audition.

Longer Strophic songs

These are similar to the verse-chorus in structure but are longer. They may have one or more verse and several choruses. Most of these songs carry a narrative: *'To Keep My Love Alive'* (Rodgers and Hart), *'The Saga of Jenny'* (Weill and Gershwin), *'Mac the Knife'* (Weill and Brecht). They are easy to work with: for the shorter version, just cut verses and choruses. Since the music remains the same for each, you can choose which verse and chorus to sing by storyline.

'The Saga of Jenny'

Here are three options for cutting *'The Saga of Jenny'*. (Weill and Gershwin) from *Lady In The Dark*. It can be found in the *Ira Gershwin Songbook* (Pub. Chappell and Co.) or *The Singer's Musical Theatre Anthology Mezzo-Soprano/Alto Vol.1* (Pub. Hal Leonard Corp.). The song is made up of an introduction, five verses (Jenny made her mind up...) with a chorus (Poor Jenny...), and a sixth verse leading into an extended coda (Jenny points a moral...).

Option 1: Start at the beginning. Sing the introduction (There once was a girl named Jenny). Then sing verse 3 with chorus (...at twenty-two), verse 5 with chorus (...at fifty-one), and verse 6 (...at seventy-five) to the end.

Option 2: (shorter) Start at the beginning. Sing the introduction (There once was a girl named Jenny), and then sing verse 2 (...when she was twelve) with the chorus. Sing verse 3 (...at twenty-two) to the line 'And then she got a husband, but he wasn't hers'. Then cut straight to 'Jenny points a moral' twenty-four bars from the end.

To do this successfully your pianist cuts a bar earlier than you ('at seventy-six') and you sing 'but he wasn't hers' all on the note G.

Option 3: (shortest) This is similar to option 2 but has an additional cut. Having arrived at 'Jenny points a moral with which you cannot quarrel, makes a lot of common sense', cut immediately to 'Anyone with vision Comes to this decision', twelve bars from the end.

Plot songs

These are structurally more complex and therefore more difficult to cut. Here are some general pointers to look out for:

1. Repeated verse sections. You may be able to use the text of only one verse and take it into the second chorus.
2. Sections of music that are a unit in themselves and so can easily be omitted. Look out for what are known as 'A', 'B' and 'C' sections. You should be able to recognise these by ear once you have heard the song through a few times, even if you don't read music. In many songs the 'A', 'B' and 'C' sections may appear more than once, usually linked by a contrasting section known as the bridge or the middle eight because traditionally it is eight bars long.
3. Codas (coda literally means 'tail-piece'). You may be able to cut from the end of a first chorus to the coda, thus being able to do your big finish.

Since many of these songs need individual attention, here are three separate examples. The first two songs have two verse sections and two 'chorus' sections. They also finish with a coda. The first song is for a man and the second for a woman.

'What am I Doin'?' from Closer Than Ever by Maltby and Shire
This song can be found in the full piano score of show (pub. Tommy Valando). It is described in detail in Chapter 9. It is a long song for auditions, and it is possible to cut it in two ways.

Option 1: Cut from the end of verse 1 to the beginning of chorus 2 (and I sit there all night in the rain, and I'm thinking.../What am I doin' up on a roof). In this version you lose the section about growing up, but the song remains powerful, if desperate.

Option 2: Start at the beginning of verse 2 (I decided that I've learned my lesson), and rely on the audience or panel to pick up the bits of the story. This works if you make the most of the words 'woman', 'crazy again', and 'tingles'. The idea that you are up on the roof becomes more shocking; it is also potentially funnier, so beware of comedy moments.

Both options 1 and 2 are perfectly acceptable musically; your job is to make the story work with half the plot missing.

Option 3 (a sixteen bar version): This is more challenging. Since the song has a great money note at the end, you may decide that that is what you want to display to the panel. In this case, start exactly sixteen bars from the end, 'What am I doin' testing her doorknob?' You have to hit the ground running!

Option 4 (another sixteen bar version): If you decide that you would rather show your narrative skills, you can start in bar 4 (the first bar you actually sing) and continue to 'sit there all night in the rain'. You are deliberately stopping in the middle of a sentence, both textually and musically, but you could make that work to your advantage: you might leave the panel wanting more. This would work extremely well if you followed the song immediately with a piece of text.

'Vanilla Ice Cream' from *She Loves Me* by Sheldon Harnick and Jerry Bock

This can be found in *The Singer's Musical Theatre Anthology Soprano Vol. II* (pub. Hal Leonard Corp.). This is a song that you might want to cut if you were using it as your second number. There is a great money note at the end, One of the main reasons for singing this song is the vocal and emotional range it demonstrates. See Chapter 9 for more details on performing it.

Option 1: Start at the very end of the first chorus at the spoken 'Where was I?' Go into the fast recitative and sing to the end. This has several advantages: if you start with 'Where was I?', you get a useful segue from being yourself speaking on stage to speaking as Amalia. Musically you include the verse, the chorus, and the money note at the end. This version shows the full range of the song (D to high B), together with comic moments and vocal display. This is a very satisfying version.

Option 2 (sixteen bars): This is much more difficult to achieve, and you will definitely need to have this written out for the pianist. You might do your speech first and follow it immediately with the song. This example is for the soprano with enormous chutzpah.

Begin at 'Where was I?' and sing the next twelve bars to 'I am so sorry about last night'. The pianist plays a B7 chord, and you then jump straight to the final 'Vanilla ice cream'. Rather than the full playout, the pianist plays a tremolo E major chord under your last word. The subtext link between 'I am so sorry about last night' and 'Vanilla ice cream' is the hardest part of this version to pull off.

'In Whatever Time We Have' from *Children of Eden* by Stephen Schwartz

This can be found in piano/vocal album *Children of Eden* (pub. Faber Music Ltd).

This song actually a duet from *Children of Eden* but can by performed as a solo by either a man or a woman. This song differs from the previous two in that there is no verse. It does, however, have several sections (some of which repeat) and a coda.

Option 1: Sing from the beginning to the end of bar 35 ('you and I will be together in whatever...') then jump straight to the last six bars ('...time we have').

Option 2: This is the same length as option 1, but with different words and slightly different music. Sing from the beginning to the end of bar 27 ('I will hold you in the dark...'). Then cut to bar 76 ('...In whatever time we have, we will make the most of time') and sing to the end.

Option 3: This is slightly longer than options 1 and 2 and includes one of the bridge sections, giving more musical and dramatic variety. Sing from the beginning to the end of bar 28 ('I will hold you in the dark...'). Then cut to the beginning of bar 60 ('We could live a hundred years...') and sing to the end.

Option 4 (short version): Start at the beginning of bar 76 ('In whatever time we have, we will make the most of time') and sing to the end. (This is actually fourteen bars long.) If you feel you want a bigger finish, you might sing the last 'whatever time we have' up an octave, although Mr Schwartz might not recommend it! He did, however, revise the score a couple of years after it opened in London, and the newer version is a little more in pop style. Look out for it.

Marking up your music

By the time you get to the audition you will have rehearsed your cuts, making sure you know which sentence links with which. However, the pianist will be seeing your cut for the first time. It is vital that your music is marked as clearly and unambiguously as possible.

Jeremy I refer to this as 'map reading'. I want to know *before* I start playing if there are any cuts, where to cut from and to, how many verses you are doing, if there is a coda, or if the music is played straight through. If you do not read music it is easy to make mistakes when indicating to the pianist which part of your song is cut; you may need help with this task before you arrive.

Remember that the pianist is reading three lines of music plus the words at once, possibly at sight. However, he will be concentrating on the two lines of the piano part. Therefore, do not just mark your cuts in the vocal line. I usually mark the beginning of a cut using a vertical opening bracket [over all three music lines, and a closing bracket] at the end of the cut section. I also strike diagonal lines through the cut sections that are clearly visible to anyone reading very fast. If you are cutting large chunks of a page, remember to strike your lines from top left to bottom right; if you only indicate a cut page with a strike from top right, the pianist may have played most of the top line of music before he realises that the page is not being used. Mark the copy with a pencil, preferably '2B', so that it is easy to read or erase if necessary. Where possible, if you are cutting more than a page of music, take it out altogether. There is nothing this pianist hates more than having to interact with pages of paper as well as to play the music.

Gillyanne Recently I was working with an actress who was falling into the trap of hunting for the right song and not completing the work on the repertoire she had. She was very attached to a song that she did well but which had pages and pages of music (including quite long piano breaks). It lasted for five minutes. She was horrified when I suggested several drastic cuts: 'But you can't do that, you're decimating the song!' she exclaimed. I reminded her that the point of the audition was to demonstrate clearly her skills as a performer to the panel, not to give a performance of the song. She got the point, and we cut the song and several others in her database.

Most music can be cut if it is well constructed, and most actors can work with the change of subtext that the cut may require. Never be afraid to make cuts if you like the song and do it well.

Chapter 12

Memorising

Learning and memorising are not the same thing. At an audition you are under extra pressure and may find it difficult to remember the words of your song. As in stage work, you will find this much easier if you think about memorising the song with all aspects of its attendant scenario and not just the words. In addition to the normal task of memorising text, you have pitch and rhythm to deal with. This is a complex task for the brain because our speech and language centre is controlled by the left brain and singing with the right brain. The right brain is responsible for our creative and intuitive side, the left for our cognitive and analytical side. So in order to memorise sung words, you must connect the brain's hemispheres. This may not present such a problem when singing in a show on stage, but in an audition you are always performing a soliloquy, so some of the cues that you might normally rely upon for memorising will be missing. Somehow you need to replace them. There are probably as many ways of memorising as there are different types of people, but it is known that people process information through their senses before sending it to the memory banks. We use information from the NLP[1] model for helping actors to learn what we have to teach them. Jeremy has found that noting which of the three primary senses (visual, auditory and kinaesthetic) are favoured by an individual is extremely useful in helping them to memorise song material.

It is important, whichever way you process information, to be accurate when first learning the lyrics or shape of a song. 'Shortcutting' by trying to get away from the page the first time through will invariably lead to learning something slightly wrong, and it is then difficult to unlearn the problem. When you come to memorise the song, you will find it valuable to play the tape with the full accompaniment and siren along to it, or listen and siren silently. This will help stimulate your auditory memory, useful in music.

[1]Neuro Linguistic Programming

Your mode

All of us use all three primary senses to process information. We tend to take in information with what in NLP is known as the 'lead' mode, and we may give out information in a second ('primary') mode. It is beyond the scope of this book to deal with the 'why' of this; those who wish to learn more about the NLP model are recommended to read *Introducing NLP* by Joseph O'Connor and John Seymour (pub. Thorsons, an imprint of Harper Collins).

Which sense for you is dominant in a learning context: visual, auditory or kinaesthetic? Do you remember things by seeing pictures in your mind, by hearing sounds in your head, or by the feel of things? Most working actors will already know their mode, even if they have never come across the NLP model, because they will have devised a way of memorising text and moving within a given spatial context. Here are some strategies for memorising music and words in the three modes:

1. Visual: run a film in your head or outside of you (make sure the images are personal to you).
2. Auditory: run a sound track internally or externally (make sure the sounds are personal to you).
3. Kinaesthetic: plot a scene (again the space can be internal or external) or remember the 'feel' of objects, people, or atmospheric conditions (make sure the spatial or touch memory is personal to you).

In all cases make your memory quite detailed.

Gillyanne My lead mode is auditory. If you are auditory biased you like to hear things to understand them. If something about hearing enables you to understand on a deeper level, auditory is your 'lead' mode of learning. I must have taught literally hundreds of students over the last eighteen years. When I meet them again I might not remember their names, but I will recall individual voice timbres quite clearly.

If auditory is your favoured mode, you are likely to be able to memorise songs quite quickly by ear. However, beware: if you do not learn melodies and rhythms accurately from the beginning, the un-learning will be tiresome because you will tend to hear in your head the sound of the line that you are anticipating in its incorrect state. Your key stimuli will be voice timbre, pitch, rhythm and tempo. What could be better when learning music?

Jeremy My lead mode is kinaesthetic. Even if I hear people demonstrating a sound, I will take it inside my head and feel what they are doing, and see the mechanics of what is happening. I also sight-read music by shapes and feel. I look for patterns (similarities and differences) rather than reading each note, which means I am able to understand complex music very quickly. In order to remember names I have to see them written down, or write them myself to lock them into my memory. I also find it helpful to write out or type words to songs that I am learning.

Gillyanne Here are some of my memorising ploys. Try them out to discover which ones work for you.

1. Paraphrase the meaning of the text.
2. Analyse the language of the text.
3. Imagine that you had to explain the meaning of the song to an audience and do so aloud.
4. Say the words out aloud without the melody. The sound of the words and the stress of the words (expression and emphasis) are part of this process. The sound of voiced consonants are particularly important to me and form part of my muscular memory.
5. Experiment with bringing the words into the memorising equation early on in the process. For me the sound of the words provide another dimension to the melody. Sequences like rhyming patterns and verse lines are important in this process. Phrase shapes and rhythmic duration are also memory triggers. Learning the words as part of the melody can make word memorising almost effortless.
6. If sections of the song appear in (or from outside of) your mind while doing other tasks (e.g. washing up, driving and so on), use this as an opportunity to rehearse the words silently. This might be done without the melody.
7. Conscious memorising can also benefit from being done in a relaxed position with the music in front of you. Silently sing the text, following the shape of the melody and rhythm. You might also sing aloud but quietly (also in a relaxed mode e.g. in the bath, lying in bed, or relaxing in a chair) and not necessarily at pitch.

Jeremy I love singing patter songs. Patter songs are often a string of thoughts (or lists) based loosely around a theme, but they can be difficult to remember in the right order. '*Mad Dogs and Englishmen*' by Noel Coward is a typical list song, and trying to remember each country and the behavioural patterns of its respective inhabitants is not easy.

Coward often uses very tasty words and relishes unusual rhymes. Each sentence will have one or two key words or phrases, and the choice phrase might be different for each person.

1. Sometimes you just need one syllable from a word: the physical impulse of the letters in that syllable can kick-start your memory.
2. Key words for memorising don't have to be the rhyming words, especially if you do not favour auditory mode! Look instead for other factors that appeal to your sense memory such as feel, taste, smell, or a physical movement.
3. Highlight your keywords and phrases in some way. Say them aloud, taste them, write them down, or draw them. You will find that a few minutes working in this way will fix whole phrases in your mind, which can be threaded together with ease.
4. Break songs down into smaller units – verses, paragraphs or sentences – to make it easier for the brain to hold information. If the song is particularly difficult to memorise, splitting the text into manageable chunks gives you the bonus of a sense of achievement each time you arrive at another landmark. You are also much more likely to discover where the problems recur, and to be able to concentrate on fixing those areas. You might even give each chunk a keyword or emotion as a title to help with ordering the chunks.

(If you are interested, you might like to spot which examples given above might belong to which mode; note the language we each used to express what we wanted to convey.)

Here are three examples of memorising in practice.

'Everybody Says Don't' from *Anyone Can Whistle* by Stephen Sondheim
Verse 1

Everybody says don't,
Everybody says don't,
Everybody says
Don't, it isn't right,
Don't, it isn't nice.
Everybody says don't,
Everybody says don't,
Everybody says
Don't walk on the grass,
Don't disturb the peace,
Don't skate on the ice.

Well, I say do!
I say walk on the grass, it was meant to feel!
I say sail!
Tilt at the windmill, and if you fail, you fail!

Everybody says don't,
Everybody says don't,
Everybody says
Don't get out of line.
When they say that, then,
Lady, that's a sign:
Nine times out of ten,
Lady you are doing just fine!

Bridge

Make just a ripple.
Come on, be brave.
This time, a ripple.
Next time, a wave.
Sometimes you have to start small,
Climbing the tiniest wall.
Maybe you're going to fall,
But it's better than not starting at all!

Verse 2

Everybody says no,
Everybody says stop,
Everybody says
Mustn't rock the boat,
Mustn't touch a thing!
Everybody says don't,
Everybody says wait,
Everybody says can't fight City Hall,
Can't upset the cart,
Can't laugh at the King!

Well, I say try!
I say laugh at the kings or they'll make you cry!
Lose your poise!
Fall if you have to,
But, lady, make a noise!

Everybody says don't,
Everybody says can't,
Everybody says
Wait around for miracles,
That's the way the world is made!

Coda

I insist on miracles, if *you* do them,
Miracles, nothing to them!
I say 'Don't': Don't be afraid!

In this song the word 'Don't' appears sixteen times. Which one leads to which line? Divide the song into paragraphs (or verses), and look for patterns in each verse. The thing to notice in this case is not where the lines are similar, but where they change.

Verse 1

Everybody says don't, don't, don't,
Everybody says don't, don't, don't,
(I say do),
Everybody says don't, don't, don't,
(When they say that, you're doing fine).

Bridge

(Come on, be brave.)

Verse 2

Everybody says no, stop, mustn't,
Everybody says don't, wait, can't,
(I say try,)
Everybody says don't, can't, wait [around]

Coda

(I insist,)

(*I* say 'don't': don't be afraid.)

Jeremy I have found that memorising is often linked with understanding. For example, notice that 'Everybody says don't' for the whole of the first verse. It is only in the second verse that they start to say other words. In one stroke you have eliminated the problem of whereabouts the words 'don't', 'no', 'can't' and so on appear. Then, analyse the changes of impulse in each sentence. For example, in my interpretation, 'Don't, it isn't right' is a mother's voice, informing and socialising a child. 'Don't get out of line' is a more pointed voice: an authority figure concerned with conforming. 'Mustn't rock the boat' is angry, whereas 'Can't fight City Hall' is wheedling and 'poor-me'. 'Wait around for miracles' is dogmatic, with a flavour of religious bigotry. You will not only colour the storyline but also the voice qualities you use. The song becomes much easier to memorise and to perform.

'Johnny One Note' from the film *Babes in Arms* by Richard Rodgers and Lorenz Hart

Jeremy The work that I did with one actor (SB) on this song showed how setting a detailed scene at the beginning of the verse can help you to remember the next five or six lines. It involved primarily visual and some kinaesthetic clues, used in the form of a film or cartoon. SB was having problems remembering not only what the words were, but also in what order she had to sing them. She was 'singing beautifully', but I was aware that she was not really involved in the text. We came up with a series of four scenes, containing all the clues to get the story in the right order.

Here are the words of the song:

Verse 1

Johnny could only sing one note and the note he sang was this:
Ah____!
Poor Johnny One Note sang out with gusto and just overloaded the place
Poor Johnny One Note yelled willy-nilly until he was blue in the face,
For holding one note was his ace.
Couldn't hear the brass,
Couldn't hear the drum,
He was in a class by himself, by gum!

Verse 2

Poor Johnny One Note got in Aida, indeed a great chance to be brave.
He took his one note, howled like the North Wind, brought forth wind that made
   critics rave, while Verdi turned round in his grave.
Couldn't hear the flute,
Or the Big Trombone,
Everyone was mute, Johnny stood alone.

Middle section

Cats and Dogs stopped yapping,
Lions in the zoo all were jealous of Johnny's big trill.

Thunderclaps stopped clapping,
Traffic ceased its roar, and they tell us Niagara stood still.
He stopped the train whistles, boat whistles, steam whistles, cop whistles,
All whistles bowed to his skill.

Verse 3

Sing Johnny One Note, sing out with gusto and just overwhelm all the crowd.
Ah___!
So sing Johnny One Note out loud.
Sing, Johnny One Note!
Sing Johnny One Note out loud!

Before the film starts, the narrator, standing next to a film screen in a studio, sets the scene in a serious tone: 'Johnny could only sing one note, and the note he sang was this', we cut to film of:

1. A close-up of Johnny's mouth, wide open, singing his one note. We pull back to see the scene: Johnny looking scared with round shoulders, singing out, filling the concert hall with sound, then yelling louder and going blue in the face, holding up a playing card (the Ace of Spades). The camera pans into the band (brass section then drums) unable to top the volume. We cut to a long shot of Johnny by himself on a massive stage.

2. Verse 2 starts with Johnny now in a breastplate striding out onto a stage past a pyramid, carrying a spear, with a wolf on a lead (for the howling). He sings his one note, and the camera cuts to audience of critics with hair streaming backwards in the gale, cheering, while to the side of the stage, a shroud (embroidered with the name 'Verdi') on a spit is slowly turning in a shallow grave. We cut to the flute and trombone players going purple trying to top the volume and then giving up.

3. The middle section takes us outside the Opera House in the rain (cue for thunderclaps later) to the zoo next door where a group of cats and dogs stop chasing each other at the sound, and a pride of mangy, depressed and wet lions sit and mumble. As the sound spreads outwards, the view goes up to the silent black skies, down to the stopped traffic, then across to a frozen Niagara Falls. Then we pan across the rail tracks to the docks where a steamboat has several policemen onboard, taking the whistles out of their mouths and hanging their heads.

4. We go back to the Opera House where a beaming Johnny is singing his head off to the crowd who stand with mouths open, stunned. And finally, we go back to the narrator, who very excited,

encourages him to carry on.

This scenario works equally well for those who favour the auditory mode (voices coming from different places in your mind's ear, together with a more vivid and complex soundtrack) or the kinaesthetic (the action happens around you with the population of the story in different places). All require you to 'set the scenes' in detail. Make sure that the detail and sense memory is personal to you. A single frame can contain an enormous amount of detail. It actually takes longer to write or tell than it does to experience.

Apart from the scenes described above, there are a couple of danger points in memorising the song. Several lines begin with either 'Poor Johnny' or 'Sing Johnny'. Notice that in the song Johnny starts off being 'Poor Johnny One Note', and ends in triumph. So 'Poor' only happens until someone has enough faith in him to give him his first job, a role in Aida! The other point to watch is the difference between 'overload' and 'overwhelms': at the beginning of the song he overloads the place, and at the end of the song he overwhelms the crowd.

The footnote to this is that, having gone through the song in this way, the next time we worked on the song, we could both remember every word and needed just thirty seconds to check the phrase order.

'I Won't Send Roses' from *Mack and Mabel* by Jerry Herman
Verse 1

I won't send roses, or hold the door.
I won't remember which dress you wore.
My heart is too much in control,
The lack of romance in my soul will turn you grey, kid,
So stay away, kid.
Forget my shoulder when you're in need.
Forgetting birthdays is guaranteed.
And if I loved you, you would be the last to know.
I won't send roses, and roses suit you so.

Verse 2

My pace is frantic, my temper's cross.
With words romantic I'm at a loss.
I'd be the first one to agree that I'm preoccupied with me,
And it's inbred, kid, so keep your head, kid.
In me you'll find things like guts and nerve,
But not the kind things that you deserve,
And so while there's a fighting chance, just turn and go.
I won't send roses, and roses suit you so.

Jeremy RN was having problems memorising this song. I decided to find out what his favoured mode of information gathering might be. It didn't help to see the words in his head, or where they were on the page. He could not hear the next phrase in his head, even when I cued certain keywords. I realised that he was a very physical performer, a kinaesthetic who processes things by how they feel to him. So rather than blocking the song broadly, I asked him to mime every word or phrase, without speaking or singing it. RN came up with several extraordinary movements that helped him get the story into his body. These included the writing of a guarantee slip for forgetting your birthday and the lining up of people to be told first about his love for you. We refined the details of his movements, and after less than five minutes he was able to recite the song almost word perfect, linking words and phrases to movements. The only phrase he struggled with was, 'I won't remember which dress you wore', as he kept changing 'which dress' to 'what dress'. His version had him standing, looking at you, pondering on the colour and shape of the frock you were wearing. I suggested that he moved forwards and flip through the racks of dresses in your wardrobe, trying to find which one it was. That change enabled him to remember the line accurately. Then I asked RN to recite the song without doing any of the movements, but to keep the muscle memory of them. He was word perfect, linking the feel of the movements in his mind to the lyrics, and incidentally having a much clearer storyline and emotional journey.

We are all of us individuals and capable of using all three of the primary senses to process and communicate information. One of the joys of working with different personalities is working out what makes memorising easier for them. A lot of our work is about making things easier. Experimentation and practice will help you to find out what works best for you.

Chapter 13

Audition Countdown

By the time you read this you will have already gone through most of
the process of audition preparation. Lets examine the steps so far:
1. By analysing what an audition is, and what it is for, you have a
   clearer idea of your role at auditions and what is expected of you
   (see Chapter 1).
2. By assessing your professional and skills levels you now have a
   realistic view of your place in the profession and can avoid the
   negative experience of unrealistic, unfulfilled expectations (see
   Chapter 2).
3. By understanding your voice type and what this may mean for
   your casting, you can avoid going to auditions that clearly call for
   a different voice type (why experience any more rejection than you
   need?) You know how to choose repertoire that will help the panel
   to see where you might 'fit' (see Chapters 3 and 4).
4. By choosing songs that suit *you*, you can demonstrate your
   strengths as a performer. Confident that you have something
   unique and special to offer, you will be less likely to fall into the
   trap of 'what must I do to make them like me?' (see Chapter 5).

The work done in these chapters only needs to be done once although
you may want to update your level of competence and skills requirements as your career develops. In addition to this you now have the
following information from Chapters 6 to 8, which you should use on
an ongoing basis:
1. The different categories of musical and types of song: these enable
   you to choose material appropriate for each audition.
2. The differences between musical styles: these help you to sing a
   song in an appropriate style.
3. A portfolio of songs categorised according to type and suitability
   to different auditions.

With these in place you can feel confident about giving the panel a
clear picture of yourself and how you might fit into their production.

Learning new songs

Each time you prepare for an audition you can only give a good account of yourself and do justice to your material if you have gone through the 'conscious learning' process. Here it is in brief:

1. Learn a song in fifteen minutes (see pages 81-3). Make sure you schedule in a learning session with a singing teacher, coach or friend who plays keyboard, in good time.
2. Get one, or preferably two rehearsal tapes of the song (see page 84).
3. Make a diction score of your song (see pages 84-9).
4. Research the context of the song (or create one that's personal to you) and make decisions about focus and play (see pages 97-107).
5. Make a map of voice qualities that reflect changes of focus and psychological states (see pages 98-100).
6. Decide if the song needs cutting (see Chapter 11).
7. Memorise the song in good time (see Chapter 12).
8. Prepare your portfolio for the audition that you plan to attend. Take out any songs that you are not prepared to sing.
9. Check the state of your music scores. Are they clearly marked up and easy for the pianist to manage? Are they well presented?

The process of conscious learning (Chapters 9 and 10) must be done each time you learn a new song. Cuts and memorising (Chapters 11 and 12) should be reviewed before each audition. Checking your portfolio and the condition of your music (Points 8 and 9) must be done before you get to the audition.

Preparing your portfolio

Having your portfolio available at the audition can work both for and against you. Sometimes it is very useful to have a back-up song, for instance, if the panel has already heard the song many times that day or if the pianist is not good. Sometimes the pianist will flip through your audition portfolio and ask you to sing a song that you really hadn't thought of doing that day. It could be a song that you don't do very well. You are very vulnerable at this point in audition: you haven't even had a chance to show what you can do and someone is suggesting you change it! Resist the temptation to please (it is after all *your* audition), and sing first what you have prepared. Make sure that you take out anything in your portfolio that you do not want to sing that day. Occasionally the panel will ask you to come up with a different song from the one you have chosen (usually this will happen with a second song) because they are looking for some other aspect in your performance. This is a time when it is to your advantage to have another one or two songs that you are happy to do, even if they are not necessarily suitable for the show. Perhaps the panel are looking for something range specific (the sopranos in *Beauty and the Beast* must be able to sing a high B easily). Or maybe they like what they have heard but need to see something more direct, dramatic, funny, or lyrical, and so on. In summary:

1. Make sure that your portfolio for the day of the audition contains one or two songs of your choice for the audition.
2. Also take an 'easy accompaniment' song.
3. Also take a song that can be sung fast or slow in case the panel ask for something faster or slower than what you are presenting.
4. Take one other song that you feel demonstrates some aspect of your skill as a performer. This need not necessarily be in the genre of the show you are auditioning for.

Care of your music

Keep your music flat. Presentation folders are a good idea for general use. If your music is crumpled, iron it so that it looks good. Get transpositions and arrangements copied out neatly, including lead sheets. And don't write on your music in anything other than pencil.

Jeremy When I am playing for auditions, I don't mind how the music is presented to me so long as I can read it, it turns easily and it doesn't fall off the stand or close when I don't want it to. So:

1. Do not take sheets of music that have not been taped together: it is simply careless and unprofessional. Not only do you run the risk of them being blown off the piano, but they can easily slide down behind the lid (on a grand) or fall between the piano and the stand (on an upright), and the pianist will have to stop.
2. Avoid taking music that has somebody else's markings on it; it is distracting to the pianist. He will do his best to follow every marking on the page, which might end up as a surprise to you if you do not follow them yourself.
3. If you are using a music book or score, make sure that it can stand open on the piano; it is extremely irritating to have to stop playing with one hand to hold a book open.

Time scale for preparation

What do we mean by 'in good time'? This depends partly on the individual artist, and partly on the management (who may not always give as much notice as they ought). Our advice is: *never* take a song that you do not know inside out to a first audition. You only have one chance to get called back, and we suggest that you don't blow it by trying to learn a song at the last minute because you do not have anything suitable. If you have been specially invited to audition for a panel who already know your work and you feel that you have nothing relevant to sing for them, take something that you are really comfortable with and offer to learn more suitable material for a recall. Sometimes you will be told at the audition that you will be recalled, but you are not given a date. The management expects at this stage that you will have suitable material to perform when they do call you. Do not be caught napping!

Our ideal timescale for learning new material for an audition is at least a week. If you have lived with a song for longer than that, better still. Some people can learn and memorise a new song in two or three days, but it cannot be done to audition standard in twenty-four hours. When asked to learn material from the show for a recall, make sure that you pull out all the stops and learn it thoroughly. At this stage the management want to know how professional and committed you are, so they will not be impressed by excuses that you 'did not have time' to learn the song properly. If you want to do a good audition, you must make time.

The four stages of competence

It would be easy to read all this information and become involved with all the things you feel you are 'not doing'. That is not the point of the book at all. Getting better results at auditions depends on you changing your attitude to them as well as changing how you prepare for them. Whenever we learn something new we go through a period of change which can be divided into four stages:

Stage 1: Unconscious incompetence (you can't manage something and don't realise it)

Stage 2: Conscious incompetence (you can't manage something and *do* realise it)

Stage 3: Conscious competence (you can now manage it but need to concentrate)

Stage 4: Unconscious competence (you can now manage it and don't need to think about it).

In Stage 1, ignorance can be bliss but may not be useful for advancing your skills level. Some of you reading this book may be only too well aware that you are unsuccessful at auditions, or feel that you 'always let yourself down', although you may not know why. This raised awareness takes you to Stage 2, which can feel temporarily uncomfortable. During this stage you *know* that something you are doing is inappropriate or inefficient. If you decide to do something about this, you will almost certainly get to Stage 3 in the cycle. At this stage you are aware of what you need to do to improve, and can do it, but you need to think consciously about it. However, you are aiming for Stage 4, where the new skill is in your muscle memory. You are able to use your new skill without having to think about it too much. Getting from Stage 3 to Stage 4 takes practise, although often you do not notice your arrival at Stage 4 until long after it has occurred. Understanding these stages of competence can be very liberating: you realise that you are at one of the middle stages of learning, rather than thinking, 'I'll never be able to get the hang of this', or 'I must be so stupid'.

You may already be aware that there is something not working about your approach to auditions. The work that we have presented in the foregoing chapters will have raised your awareness to certain aspects that may be lacking in your preparation of material, to unclear goals and other forms of self-sabotage that affect your performance at audition. If you have followed the instructions and exercises, you will already have gained a great deal of knowledge about your skills and strengths, and the areas you need to work on. Some of these new skills will need concentration to achieve, but this need not stop you from doing auditions. After a short while, the process of preparation will be automatic and just a normal part of your professional life. You can use the four stages of competence to help you in the learning of any new task or the taking on of information.

Nerves and stage fright

People often ask about nerves and what to do about them. It's the day of your audition. You wake up feeling keyed up. As the day goes on and you get nearer to the time you start to feel sick. Or perhaps you are standing in a long queue waiting to collect a ticket so that you can get a number to be heard some three hours later. This is a familiar scenario. Here's the good news: Nerves are a positive part of performing. They can heighten your awareness and increase your speed of response, enabling you to give your best on cue. But what if nerves get the better of you?

Ten possible causes of stage fright

1. Is the repertoire right for me?
2. Is my voice right for this song?
3. Have I got the skills needed for this job?
4. Will I show myself in a good light?
5. Is the repertoire right for the job?
6. Is the pianist good or bad?
7. Will I remember the words?
8. Will I remember when to come in?
9. Will the panel like me?
10. Will I get the job?

If you have been working through the information in this book, you will already have tools to deal with most of these fears. You will know that your voice is right for the songs in your portfolio, and that those songs all fall in your *FOAL* area. You will already know your own levels of competence and can match them to the job. Because you are confident with your choice of repertoire and your understanding of the characters, you will know that you are able to demonstrate your strengths and give a good account of yourself. By finding out as much as possible about the type of piece you are auditioning for, you will have identified the style of the piece and the type of songs required. Even though each audition may have a different pianist, you are confident that you have given him/her every pointer in assisting you in your performance. You also have a song in your repertoire with a simpler accompaniment if you feel he/she is not up to playing your song. Having learned your repertoire using the 'Learn A Song In Fifteen Minutes' technique, you will know how the music, words and rhythms fit together. You will understand where your musical entries fit and will have memorised the song in a way that is appropriate to you. Although the panel may change for each audition (or even each recall) you are comfortable with them because you are confident in your abilities, and know that you can present yourself in the best light for you. You know that they are extremely keen to cast the role, and you are aware that it is less important that they like you than that they think of you as competent.

This leaves us with point 10. Here's a reminder of what we said at the end of Chapter 1:

1. When going to any audition, be sure of what it is that you have to offer before you go.
2. If you are doing the audition to get feedback about yourself, your skills or your professional level, don't go because you will not get it!

The point of doing an audition is to get employment. It is also a job opportunity that in many cases can extend beyond the musical you are auditioning for. If you do a good audition it will not go unnoticed. Members of the panel may invite you to be seen for other projects they are involved in, or pass your name on to other managements. The very least that can happen is that someone who heard you that day will remember you next time. You already have a head-start.

Chapter 14

At The Audition

In Chapter 1 we talked about the special conditions of auditioning and why it is a unique experience for theatre performers (performing with a complete stranger, with no audience in an empty theatre that you can see, alone on stage, in front of people who are there to judge what you are doing and so on).

Almost everything that happens from the moment you are called to audition (or make a decision to attend an open call) to the moment after you leave could be summed up in three points:

1. Be professional.
2. Be professional.
3. Be professional.

As part of our own preparation for this chapter we ran a series of interviews with agents, casting directors and musical directors concerning their expectations and experiences of auditions: professional behaviour and commitment came at the top of everyone's list.

Here are some general points about what to expect when you go to an audition.

Open calls

Auditions average between three and ten minutes. Recalls might be longer, especially if the director wants to work with you; it could be as long as twenty minutes.

When you attend an open audition you have very little time to show what you can do. It is fair to say that open calls are sometimes used as publicity exercises for the production or production company concerned. That is the worst case scenario. Some of the larger production companies use the open calls to find out what's 'out there'. Open calls can be a way to get experience of how you hold up at auditioning or a way to get onto somebody's list for possible audition calls when you do not have representation. Expect to sing a short song or sixteen bars at one of these events and to stand in line for a long time. Do not try to do anything elaborate for this type of audition. Take exactly the kind of music that has been asked for, dress smartly, and be totally on the ball. Do not expect eye contact, smiles and chit-chat, the panel are seeing four hundred people that day and they do not have time.

Private auditions and recalls

Usually a first private audition lasts about five to ten minutes. You might be asked to bring two contrasting songs, or a song and a speech. Alternatively you may be asked to bring one song and expected to be read a piece of text or a scene as for a casting. Make sure that you have done your research on the part you are being seen for. Either your agent or the representative of the casting director will be able to brief you on this. PCR is also a useful source of information. Casting directors indicated that for a first audition they want to hear you sing music of your own choice in an appropriate musical genre. The song or songs chosen should demonstrate your vocal range. (This means not your total range but your voice type and comfort zone.)

Recalls can vary in their requirements. Always try to find out what the panel would like from you on the recall. Rather than feeling pressured by the recall, you can relax in the knowledge that you have already passed the test of being professionally at the right level for the show. Make sure that you continue to be professional and learn thoroughly any music that is sent to you. Third and subsequent calls to audition are all opportunities for you to show more of yourself as a performer and cast member. The latter can be very important: most directors and musical directors want to work with people who are pleasant and professional. Across the board casting directors and agents urged that in second and subsequent calls you be prepared to make bold acting choices, rather than playing safe. It is a mistake to try to second-guess what the creative team may want because you want to please. Do your job as an actor and leave them to do theirs.

Multiple recalls

Currently these are tending to become the norm in the UK. For musicals in the West End anything between five and nine recalls is not unusual. Reasons for this vary. Long running musicals have contracts to sort out with existing cast. Productions that are transferring from abroad (for example the USA) will have a separate creative team who will come in after the initial round of casting, and that can make the overall process lengthy. Musicals are a complex art form, and new musicals may go through many changes before getting to the production stage. Inevitably there are casualties in the casting process as things evolve. You need to be highly pragmatic in your attitude to these situations and not take it personally. In the American system, actors are paid a percentage of the equity minimum for attending auditions after the third recall.

Manner of dress

In general terms this means looking smart and personable; your dress does not have to be formal. If you are going for a specific role it is helpful to wear something that will enable the panel to see you playing that character. This doesn't mean you have to wear period costume, but it does mean that if you are going up for, say, Anne in *A Little Night Music*, that you should wear something young and feminine. Avoid wearing uncomfortable shoes or anything that you have not worn before. Girls should make sure that their hair is dressed so that the panel can see their faces. If you wear glasses and these are not on your photograph, you might consider taking them off for the duration of the performance.

Your CV and photograph

Always have these with you, even if they are not asked for in advance. Discuss with your agent how your CV (resumé) should look, and do not be afraid to reformat it when going up for different types of audition. This is easy to do nowadays with modern technology.

Waiting in the wings

For some people the period of waiting in the green room is the most dangerous time for their confidence. You might feel that you are surrounded by actors who are 'more attractive, more talented, more *right* for the part than me'. Beware of trying to decide at this time what the panel might want. One actress we work with almost ruined an audition for a pantomime because she had prepared a song for the juvenile lead part, and walked into a room full of wicked fairies. She went into the classic 'have I brought the right song?' worry, and she had to work very hard to pull her audition mindset back. It did not occur to her that she might have been the only juvenile lead auditionee invited that day. The golden rule in the waiting area is that everybody *always* looks fitter, more attractive, better dressed, more castable, and sings better, higher, louder and longer than you do. Accept it and smile; everybody else will see exactly the same in you.

Sometimes other auditionees indulge in one-upmanship. This falls into several categories: warming up loudly coupled with 'mine's bigger than yours', the 'my last film with *dear dear so and so* was so wonderful', or the 'what are *you* doing here?' coupled with 'oh, you don't want to sing that'. Some actors are more aware of what they are doing than others, but generally the apparent put-down is not deliberate. It is usually an attempt to deal with the horrors of potential rejection in front of your peers. After all, the very best audition would be one in which no-one else is auditioning. If you tend to feel demoralised by these antics, take a book (you don't have to be actually reading it), sit in the toilets, or arrive early, register and then wait just outside the building. If you follow some of the audition warm-up exercises, you will be too focussed to get involved.

Staying grounded

When we feel nervous we tend to close up inside; our pulse quickens and our breathing pattern alters. Rather than trying to control the breath and the shakiness we naturally feel as a result of chemical changes in the body, it is good to have something to do. Here are some practical strategies that we suggest to clients who are waiting in the wings:

1. Use the sirening exercise that is described on page 21: it will keep your voice on the boil in a non-intrusive way and keep you in touch with your vocal mechanism.
2. If your throat his tightened up and you feel dry this is a result of constriction in the larynx, a natural part of our flight-and-fight response. By chuckling and laughing silently we can overcome this urge to constrict. You can even chuckle gently out loud and you will feel a difference. Use the laugh techniques for a few minutes at a time and then allow your breathing pattern to return to normal, while still pretending to laugh.

   To steady your body (rather than the breath) 'anchoring' techniques are recommended. These can also be performed silently and will help you to feel strong and grounded.

3. One of the anchoring techniques is to pull up at the back of the neck as you straighten the cervical spine. You can also firm up the spaces inside the mouth by rehearsing silently the beginning of a sneeze. Keep that feeling of 'lift' inside the mouth and at the back of the neck and allow your breathing pattern to return to normal. Repeat the siren at

this stage.

Another useful anchoring technique works more of the whole body.

4. If you are sitting on a chair, put your hands underneath the chair and make as if to pull you and the chair up. (You can't, of course). Relax your shoulders as you do this and check that your spine is in alignment. Notice how strong this makes you feel in the torso area. Use it as you look around you and breathe gently and slowly.

The combination of the anchoring techniques with that of the silent laugh enables you to connect with positive sensations. You will still feel nervous but you will also feel ready. Repeat this sequence and the sirening at intervals of your waiting period as often as you need to. If you are unfamiliar with these techniques you can read about them in greater detail in *Singing and The Actor*.

Both of us use Educational Kinesiology (colloquially known as Brain Gym®) during workshops and as a preparation for our own seminar work. The exercises to help us and our clients to integrate and coordinate learning and performing. Dr Paul E. Denison has written several good books on the subject of brain integration and whole brain learning. If you take a workshop with someone who teaches the Brain Gym ® techniques you will probably be given some exercises specific to you and your physiology.

Taking your space

When you go to an audition you go in as yourself, leave as yourself and in the interim may be playing one or two roles. Recognising this as a task is half the battle of being able to manage getting in and out of character. Actors doing a singing audition often have a short play in that enables them to focus in on the story of the song. There are one or two things you can do here to make sure that you stay in charge of this process.

1. Practise doing the song as for audition in at least one of your coaching sessions. This includes talking the pianist through the map-reading, moving into the performing space and focussing down during the play-in.
2. Give clear messages to the pianist when you are ready to start. A nod or glance is fine once you are in position. We realise that this is difficult in an unknown space.
3. As you walk in and greet or are greeted, consciously look around at the space. Assess a good position for your song, one that you are comfortable with.
4. As you move from the pianist to the performing space, focus on it

and then stand quietly for a moment in it, indicating 'in neutral' with your body language. If the pianist is at all sensitive he or she will know that you are not ready. At that point one of the panel may say 'when you are ready' (subtext: we are ready for you now!), and you can make your indication to the pianist.

When you have completed your song you may find it helpful to go back into a neutral stance for a moment, even if you are between songs. When you are finished it is usual for the panel to say something (even if it is only 'thanks' and 'goodbye'), and you might then move your eye focus around the room again.

Where is your eye focus at an audition?

Young students often ask if they should or shouldn't look at the panel while performing their song. It is inappropriate to sing your song to the panel, they are not interested in interacting with you during performance, though they may well be afterwards. If you have planned your work you will know how large your space is for the world of the song and who might be in that space with you (see Chapter 10). Audition spaces can vary from a room that is ten by ten feet to Drury Lane. Pack a mental zoom lens with you so that your personal performing space is able to fit the dimensions of any room or theatre.

Duetting with a stranger: dealing with the pianist

Jeremy Audition pianists are highly skilled musicians who are working with you on many levels. While they are reading, they will be listening for what you are doing, and also anticipating what you will be doing in the next sentence. I find it extremely easy to accompany someone whose thought processes are clear, even if it is a reading I have never heard before.

Your partner in performance will need two key pieces of information from you (no more): the speed and feel, and the map-reading. When you hand him (or her) your music (open at the right page), show him quickly if there are any cuts and where they start and finish. Also explain, if relevant, whether you are doing all the verses and any 'back to the beginning then to the coda' instructions. That will take fifteen seconds. Then give him the speed and feel of the piece in general, and let him know if there are sections at different speeds. That should take you about thirty seconds. Most panels will allow you this time as they do not want you to have to stop for musical errors once you have started.

When I am coaching people on dealing with the pianist, I always tell them not to indicate the speed by singing the first bars of the tune. It is very rare for a singer to settle into the speed until several bars in. The most successful method is to sing a bar somewhere in the middle of the chorus, preferably one that has more words and shorter notes. If you sing your busiest bar, you are more likely to hit the speed you want. In '*This Is the Moment*' for example, I would choose the following bars of music as a guide.

Beware of singing the tune under your breath to the pianist. Almost every time an actor has given me the speed under their breath, it has been far too fast. Occasionally in a workshop I will actually play the speed the actor has indicated under their breath; it's usually a shock. While you may not wish the panel to hear you until you are ready, it is better to sing aloud. The panel know the difference between your performance and your preparation.

In addition to a tempo guide, I recommend that singers give a (one-phrase) guide to the feel of a piece. Simple instructions such as 'moving forward', 'held back', 'rock feel', 'lazy' are helpful to the pianist to put your speed in context. Finally, a good pianist listens particularly hard when you sing your first line to see if the speed he has set is comfortable for you. It's the easiest time to change what he is doing, so take the bull by the horns and sing faster (or slower) if it is not as you want it.

Taking charge

Be pleasant and professional when you are introduced to or greet the panel. Sometimes people will give you eye contact when you are performing, sometimes not. It is important that the panel keeps focussed on their job, and this may involve paper shuffling and conversation, all of which can be off-putting. Remember that you are not performing to them but for them. Focus on being as real as you can in your world of the song.

1. If you have two songs and the panel ask which one you would like to sing first, don't be 'polite' and say you don't mind. Take charge of your own audition and choose!

2. Sometimes you will be asked to stop before the end of your song. This is fine; it just means that the panel has heard all that is needed in order to make a decision. Heart-breaking though it may be when you have spent days (weeks even) preparing for this moment, do not let it put you off but gracefully come back into being you and take your cue from them.

3. If the pianist plays your song at totally the wrong speed it is best to stop him or her politely as soon as you can. Simply indicate again the speed you would like and start again. Other than indicating when you are ready to start do not look at the pianist during your song. Repeated glancing at the pianist reveals that you are insecure with your material and therefore improperly prepared. Do *not* glare at him as if the entire world is his fault. He won't like it, and the panel will not have any sympathy for you.

4. If you dry, pick up as quickly as you can. The pianist will usually cue you in so it is OK to look over at this moment.

5. Sometimes the panel will want to talk with you. This is usually because they want to get a feel for you as a person. Just be yourself and act professionally.

6. Sometimes the panel will ask you to sing a scale in order to test your range. Take a few moments to collect yourself if this happens, rather than rushing in. There may well be some aspect of this that you can take charge of; perhaps you could request singing on your favourite vowel or humming the notes before you sing them aloud. (We would recommend sirening.)

7. Sometimes you will be asked to repeat a section of your song in another mode. Typical examples are 'would you sing that in chest or head voice?' or 'could you sing in the manner of this or that character?' Make sure you understand the instructions before you attempt the repeat. If in doubt, ask.

8. If the pianist asks you to do a song other than the one you have brought, resist. It is your audition. Be polite but firm. The only exception to this rule is if the pianist is also the musical director of the show (as sometimes happens on smaller productions).

9. If the panel ask you to sing something other than the song or songs of your choice try to find out why. If there is a good reason, offer to sing one of the other songs you have brought with you that day. If there is not, say that you really would like them to hear one that you prepared for today first. (Usually this happens because not all the panel is agreed on the criteria for the audition, e.g. the choreographer and the director have different ideas. Don't let this sabotage your audition.)

If you are going to be an actor, singer or dancer, auditioning will be part of your professional life. Auditions are rarely easy, what makes the difference is how you handle them. Almost everything that is needed to make a successful audition happens before you walk through the door. Performances that 'work' do so as a result of the performer making and carrying out various decisions. By making decisions beforehand, you can remain in control. Good luck, and enjoy your auditioning.

Appendix A

Stage I. The Interview

Using the chart at the end of the appendix, fill in your answers to the following list of questions. You may not have answers to all of the questions, and some may be easier to answer than others. Note which ones you can give instant or multiple answers to, as this can be as important as your actual answers. Also write down any examples of things you hate in the list: your strong dislikes can give valuable information about the areas that have resonance for you. You may find it easier to do this with the help of a friend. Only after you have answered all the questions should you proceed with the analysis.

1. Who are your favourite stand-up comedians? Are there any you strongly dislike?
2. What are your favourite sitcoms or comedy programmes?
3. What are your favourite TV/radio dramas, named (e.g. *Inspector Morse*) or by genre (e.g. detective)?
4. What are your favourite soaps or long-running dramas? Are there any you hate?
5. What other types of programming do you like (e.g. documentaries, nature programmes, arts programmes, etc)?
6. What are your favourite films?
7. What are your favourite books?
8. Who are your favourite actors (male or female)? Are there any you strongly dislike?
9. What are your favourite theatre pieces, named (e.g. *King Lear*) or by genre (e.g. Shakespearean tragedies)?
10. What music do you like? Separate between active listening and background or mood-enhancing.
11. What are your hobbies, sports or physical activities? Are there any types you strongly dislike?
    Answers at Stage I might look like this:

Stage I. The Interview	Stage IIa. Type	Stage IIb. Essence
1. *Victoria Wood*		
1. *Eddie Izzard*		
2. *Dislike sitcoms*		
3. *Miss Marple Investigates*		
3. *Bob and Rose*		
3. *Dislike Cracker*		
etc		

Stage IIa. Type

The top layer of information identifies the genre from which an answer comes, and the general type within the genre. Describe each of your answers *in one phrase* (imagine talking to a friend who isn't familiar with them). We have given you some examples to start you off.

Comedians: stand-up train-of-thought, stand-up physical, stand-up joke telling, stand-up situation, comedy character

Sitcoms: domestic, relationship, surreal, character sketch, language-based

TV drama: contemporary, period, comedy-drama, gritty, crime, serial, children's, long-running sequential, science fiction

TV soaps: dramatic highs and lows, ordinary, down-to-earth, fast-moving storylines, slow build

Other TV: nature programmes, travel programmes, current affairs, documentary, historical, children's programming, informational, lifestyle, entertainment, chat show, game show

Books: thrillers, legal or courtroom, adventure, sci-fi, biography, romantic, classics, historical novels, non-fiction, self-development, new-age

Films: current, period, comedy, gritty, crime, children's, cartoons (animation), blockbusters, Bollywood

Actors: leading man, character, comedy actor, strong character

Theatre: naturalistic, fantastical, theatrical, conversational, modern, restoration

Music-type of listening: active (the music has your full attention); passive (background music to other tasks such as driving, at work, or socialising)

Type of music: classical orchestral, instrumental, vocal recital, vocal opera, choral, early music, world music, New Age, easy listening, jazz vocal, jazz instrumental, country, gospel, soul or blues, pop (anything from Motown and disco to garage and gangsta)

Hobbies: crafts (needlework, marquetry, pottery, DIY), visual (jigsaws, painting), visual competitive (computer games), physical competitive (football, tennis), physical non-competitive (yoga, aerobics), outdoor pursuits (canoeing, mountain biking, hiking), collecting (antiques, philately)

Here is our example with Stage IIa completed:

Stage I. The Interview	Stage IIa. Type	Stage IIb. Essence
1. Victoria Wood	Stand-up situation	
1. Eddie Izzard	Stand-up train-of-thought	
2. Dislike sitcoms	Situations with audience	
3. Miss Marple Investigates	Murder mystery	
3. Bob and Rose	Relationship drama	
3. Dislike Cracker	Crime drama	
etc		

Stage IIB. Essence

Now describe to your friend the 'subtext' – the feel or flavour – of each example: warmth, style, approach, detail, power of drama, depth of characterisation, character type, emotional overtones. This becomes the second layer of analysis: the Essence.

Here are some example words:

Sarcastic, soft-edged, off-the-wall, slapstick, witty, creative, hard-line, blue, political, satirical, bittersweet, romantic, subversive, epic,

action, suspense, intelligent, philosophical, comic, cathartic, escapist, surreal, gritty, wide-angle, close detail, current, historical, people or buildings/land based, investigative, light-hearted, cheesy, basic, clever, outrageous, intricate, relationship, philosophical, spiritual, uplifting, depressing, life-changing, percipient, informative, exciting, gripping, calming, arousing, energised.

Here is our example with Stage IIb completed:

Stage I. The Interview	Stage IIa. Type	Stage IIb. Essence
1. Victoria Wood	Stand-up situation	Warm, domestic, witty
1. Eddie Izzard	Stand-up train of thought	Bizarre, surreal, witty
2. Dislike sitcoms	Situations with audience	Hate canned laughter, brainless
3. Miss Marple Investigates	Murder mystery	Period, quaint, detailed
3. Bob and Rose	Relationship drama	Warm, slightly controversial
3. Dislike Cracker	Crime drama	Too violent and gory
etc		

Stage III. Your Profile

Take your list of words and look for trends: similarities and strong differences. Things that appear to be contradictory can be very useful in finding your *FOAL* area. This should shorten your list, and you can then précis what remains into five or six key phrases. It is important when analysing your answers that you don't look for trends until you have finished answering all the questions.

In our short example warm and witty, domestic and detailed appear, together with surreal, quaint and slightly controversial; gory and violent are not liked, together with the mindless aspect of 'being told when to laugh'. Therefore the *FOAL* Profile might read '**warm and witty but with a twist, detailed but not clinical (gory), independent**'.

Stage 1. The Interview							Stage IIa. Type							Stage IIb. Essence						

Index

Anchoring 135–6
Audition Types 4–5
Backphrasing and Rubato
  63–5
Ballad 54
Ballad
  Dramatic Ballad 54
  Rock or Pop Ballad 55
  Swing Ballad 55
  Torch song 54
  Waltz Ballad 55
Brain Gym ® 136
Casting, Physical Type 32–3
Competence, Four Stages of
  128–9
Competence Level 8
  Actor-musician 13–14
  Actor-singer 10–12
  Booth-singer 16–17
  Dancer-singer 12–13
  Singer-actor 15–16
  Singer-dancer 14–15
  Swing 18
  Work arena 17–18
Cuts
  Plot Songs 110
  Strophic Songs 109
  Verse-chorus songs 108
Database
  building 48–9
  discarding songs 75
Decay 64–5
Diction Score 84–9
Duetting with a Stranger 137

Dynamic Control 22
Fach 32
FOAL Process 38–48,141–7
Focus
  House 98
  Internalised 98
  Unifocus 97
  Vanilla Ice Cream 10
  What am I Doin'? 106
Function, the five W's 94–7
Healthy Voice 22–3
Key 89–90
Landscaping 65
Learn a Song in 15 Minutes
  81–3, 126
Making the most of you 37
Memorising
  your mode 116
  Mirening 83
Music
  Care 127
  Marking up 114
Music Score 89–92
Musical
  Cabaret 52
  Classic Book 52
  Concept 52
  Movie 52
  Seven Categories of 50
  Sketch 51
  Tribute 51
  Verismo 50
Musical Cues
  Vanilla ice cream 102

What am I doin'? 106
Nerves and Stage fright 129–30
NLP 116
Orchestrations 66
PCR 53, 133
Performable unit 108
Phrasing 62–4
Pitching and Tuning 20
Play 100
Portfolio, deciding on 75
Range
    assessing actual range 20–2
    assessing Comfort Zone
        26–30
    assessing working range
        22, 27–30
    Baritone expected working
        29
    Bass expected working 29
    Contralto expected working
        28
    Mezzo expected working 27
    Soprano expected working
        27
    Tenor expected working 28
Rehearsal Tapes 84

Rhythm and Pitch 59–60
Siren 21
Staying Grounded 135–7
Style
    changing orchestrations
        67–70
    Moments In the Woods 100
    This Is the Moment 59–65
    Vocal 70
Success, Measuring 6
Swing 17–18
Taking Charge 138
Tempo and Feel 66
Tessitura 26, 65
Transposing your song 90–2
Uptempo 55
Uptempo
    Dramatic uptempo 57
    Patter Song 56
    Point number 56
    Swing and ragtime 56
True up tempo 56
Voice Clinic 23
Voice Qualities 23–4, 100
Voice Qualities, Changing 71–2
Word Shaping 60–2

Index of Song Titles

'A Trip To The Library' (She Loves Me) 77-80
'American Dream' (Miss Saigon) 56
'And the World Goes Round' (New York, New York) 54
'Another Day/Glory' (Rent) 49
'Another Hundred People' (Company) 56
'At the End of the Day' (Les Misérables) 57
'At Times Like This' (Lucky Stiff) 48
'Be On Your Own' (Nine) 57
'Being Alive' (Company) 54
'Blame It On A Summer Night' (Rags) 48
'Broadway Baby' (Follies) 69
'Bui-Doi' (Miss Saigon) 49
'But Not For Me' (Girl Crazy / Crazy For You) 76-80, 110
'Can You Feel the Love Tonight?' (The Lion King) 55
'Cats are Purrfect' (Dick Whittington) 77-80
'Cheer up Charlie' (Charlie and The Chocolate Factory) 49
'Child of Newgate' (Moll Flanders) 34
'Christmas Lullaby' (Songs For a New World) 49
'Comedy Tonight' (A Funny Thing Happened On The Way To The
Forum) 98
'Could I Leave You?' (Follies) 77-80
'Crossword Puzzle' (Starting Here Starting Now) 56
'Daddy's Hands' (Ragtime) 67
'Dance a Little Closer' (Dance A Little Closer) 55
'Dance Ten, Looks Three' (A Chorus Line) 12
'Dear Friend' (She Loves Me) 34
'Delilah' (by Mason & Smith) 54
'Don't Rain on My Paradev' (Funny Girl) 34
'Empty Chairs at Empty Tables' (Les Misérables) 49
'Everybody Says Don't' (Anyone Can Whistle) 118-21
'Fear No More the Heat o' the Sun' (Cymbeline) 11
'Fools Songs' (King Lear)11
'Funny' (Funny Girl) 31
'God on High' (Les Misérables) 54, 97

'Good Thing Going' (Merrily We Roll Along) 49
'Greased Lightning' (Grease) 56
'Habañera' (Carmen Jones) 68
'Happily Ever After' (Once Upon A Mattress) 34
'Herod's Song' (Jesus Christ Superstar)56
'Hold On' (The Secret Garden) 49, 77-80
'Holding To the Ground' (Falsettos) 77-80
'Home' (Beauty and the Beast) 49
'How Did I End Up Here?' (Romance Romance) 57
'I Cain't Say No' (Oklahoma!) 56
'I Can Cook Too' (On The Town) 34
'I Don't Know How to Love Him' (Jesus Christ Superstar) 55
'I Get A Kick Out of You' (Anything Goes) 109
'I Hear Bells' (Starting Here Starting Now) 77-80
'I Take My Chances' (by Mary-Chapin Carpenter and Don Schlitz) 77-80
'I Think I May Want to Remember Today' (Starting Here Starting Now) 56, 69-70
'I Who Have Nothing' (by Mogol & Donida, Lieber & Stoller) 54
'I Will Always Love You' (sung by Whitney Houston) 55
'I Will Survive' (sung by Gloria Gaynor)110
'I Won't Send Roses' (Mack and Mabel) 123-4
'I'm Not Getting Married Today' (Company) 56
'If' (Two On The Aisle) 56
'If I Loved You' (Carousel) 58
'If I Sing' (Closer Than Ever) 49
'If you go away' (by Jacques Brel) 54
'If You Want To Die In Bed' (Miss Saigon) 57, 98
'I'm Breaking Down' (Falsettos) 77-80
'In Whatever Time We Have' (Children of Eden) 49, 113
'Isn't It Romantic?' (Love Me Tonight) 110
'Isn't This A Lovely Day?' (Top Hat) 109
'It Needs Work' (City of Angels) 77-80
'It's An Art' (Working) 77-80
'Johnny One Note' (Babes In Arms) 56, 121-3
'Learn Your Lessons Well' (Godspell) 56
'Liaisons' (A Little Night Music) 28
'Look What Happened to Mabel' (Mack and Mabel) 97
'Luck Be a Lady' (Guys and Dolls) 56
'Mac The Knife' (Threepenny Opera) 110
'Mad Dogs and Englishmen' (Words and Music) 117
'Master of the House' (Les Misérables) 56, 98
'Meadowlark' (The Baker's Wife) 54

152

'Miss Byrd' (Closer Than Ever) 56
'Moments in the Woods' (Into the Woods) 76-80, 94-100
'Music Of The Night' (Phantom of the Opera) 91
'My Friends' (Sweeney Todd) 54
'My Funny Valentine' (Babes in Arms) 76-80, 109
'My Heart Belongs To Daddy' (Leave It To Me) 110
'Naughty Baby' (Crazy For You) 76-80
'Nice Work If You Can Get It' (Lady Be Good / Damsel in Distress) 49
'No Business Like Show Business' (Annie Get Your Gun) 56
'Not a Day Goes By' (Merrily We Roll Along) 65
'Nothing' (A Chorus Line) 56
'Now' (A Little Night Music) 56
'Oklahoma!' (Oklahoma!) 56
'One More Kiss' (Follies) 55
'Our Love is Here to Stay' (The Goldwyn Follies) 109
'Our Time' (Merrily We Roll Along) 49
'Out of My Dreams' (Oklahoma!) 55, 97
'Proud Lady' (The Baker's Wife) 57
'Remember' (A Little Night Music) 55
'Saga Of Jenny' (Lady in the Dark) 77-80
'Send in the Clowns' (A Little Night Music) 97
'Shy' (Once Upon a Mattress) 77-80
'So Many People In the World' (Marry Me A Little) 82
'Someone to Watch Over Me' (Oh, Kay!) 56, 69
'Stand By Me' (Smokey Joe's Café) 58
'Sun and Moon' (Miss Saigon) 31
'Take It On The Chin' (Me and My Girl) 77-80
'Tell My Father' (The Civil War) 49
'Ten Minutes Ago' (Cinderella) 55
'The Girls of Summer' (Marry Me a Little) 55
'The Man that Got Away' (A Star Is Born) 54
'The Reason' (sung by Celine Dion) 55
'The Saga Of Jenny' (Lady In The Dark) 110-11
'The Trolley Song' (Meet Me In St Louis) 56
'The Wages Of Sin' (The Mystery of Edwin Drood) 77-80
'There are worse things I could do' (Grease) 54
'They All Laughed' (Shall We Dance?) 110
'This Is the Moment' (Jekyll and Hyde) 59, 71, 82, 138
'Those Magic Changes' (Grease) 31
'Threepenny Opera' - Second Act Finale 57
'Time Heals Everything' (Mack and Mabel) 85
'To Keep My Love Alive' (A Connecticut Yankee In The Court of

King Arthur) 110
'*Two People In Love*' (*Baby*) 49, 56
'*Unusual Way*' (*Nine*) 82
'*Use What You Got*' (*The Life*) 98
'*Vanilla Ice Cream*' (*She Loves Me*) 34, 100-4, 112-13
'*What am I Doin'?*' (*Closer Than Ever*) 98, 104-7, 111- 12
'*What Did I Have That I Don't Have?*' (*On a Clear Day*) 77-80
'*What I Did For Love*' (*A Chorus Line*) 65
'*What More Do I Need?*' (*Marry Me A Little*) 31
'*Where am I Going?*' (*Sweet Charity*) 98
'*Where Do Broken Hearts Go?*' (sung by Whitney Houston) 59
'*Wherever he ain't*' (*Mack and Mabel*) 56
'*Whistle Down the Wind*' (*Whistle Down the Wind*) 55, 72
'*Who Is This Man?*' - Javert's suicide (*Les Misérables*) 54
'*With So Little To Be Sure Of*' (*Anyone Can Whistle*) 85-9
'*Worst Pies In London*' (*Sweeney Todd*) 77-80

Song Credits

Everybody Says Don't
Words and Music by Stephen Sondheim
© 1973 Burthen Music Co Inc, USA
Warner/Chappell Music Ltd, London W6 8BS
Reproduced by permission of International
Music Publications Ltd
All Rights Reserved.

(I Think) I May Want To Remember Today
Words by Richard Maltby Jr
Music by David Shire
© 1969 Maltby-Shire Productions Inc and
Chappell & Co Inc, USA
Warner/Chappell Music Ltd, London W6 8BS
Reproduced by permission of International
Music Publications Ltd
All Rights Reserved.

I Won't Send Roses
Words and Music by Jerry Herman
© 1944 Jerryco Music Co and Edwin H
Morris & Co Inc, USA
Chappell Morris Ltd, London W6 8BS
Reproduced by permission of International
Music Publications Ltd
All Rights Reserved.

Johnny One Note
Words by Lorenz Hart
Music by Richard Rodgers
© 1981 Chappell & Co Inc, USA
Warner/Chappell Music Ltd, London W6 8BS
Reproduced by permission of International
Music Publications Ltd
All Rights Reserved.

Moments In The Woods
Words and Music by Stephen Sondheim
© 1988 Rilting Music Inc, USA
Warner/Chappell Music Ltd, London W6 8BS
Reproduced by permission of International
Music Publications Ltd
All Rights Reserved.

The Saga Of Jenny
Words by Ira Gershwin
Music by Kurt Weill
© 1940 Chappell & Co Inc and the Kurt Weill
Foundation For Music Inc, USA
Warner/Chappell Music Ltd, London W6 8BS
Reproduced by permission of International
Music Publications Ltd
All Rights Reserved.

So Many People
Words and Music by Stephen Sondheim
© 1973 Chappell & Co Inc, USA
Warner/Chappell Music Ltd, London W6 8BS
Reproduced by permission of International
Music Publications Ltd
All Rights Reserved.

Unusual Way
Words and Music by Maury Yeston
© 1975 Yeston Music Ltd and EMI
Harmonies Ltd, USA
Worldwide print rights controlled by Warner
Bros. Publications Inc/IMP Ltd
Reproduced by permission of International
Music Publications Ltd
All Rights Reserved

What Am I Doin'
Words by Richard Maltby Jr
Music by David Shire
© 1991 Revelation Music Publishing Co and
Fiddleback Music Publishing Co, .USA
Warner/Chappell Music Ltd, London W6 8BS
Reproduced by permission of International
Music Publications Ltd
All Rights Reserved.

With So Little To Be Sure Of
Words and Music by Stephen Sondheim
© 1973 Burthen Music Co Inc, USA
Warner/Chappell Music Ltd, London W6 8BS
Reproduced by permission of International
Music Publications Ltd
All Rights Reserved.